Before you start reading, please give me a minute

This is a simple happiness scale, mark your present level of happiness on this 0 to 10 level scale.

Thanks

This book is dedicated to my beloved dad, to me who is a live example of wining spirit. He has tremendous ability to win obstacles.

He, through the examples of his life, has taught me how to relish life even during the period of struggle and sacrifice. To me he is a symbol of ideal mankind and an absolute powerhouse. Though he now lives miles away, yet I feel his presence every moment.

I salute him for his guidance and magnificent efforts to implant seeds of wining attitudes in my tender mind.

Feel Good Factors of Life

Ten Commandments for Feeling Better and Marching Towards Success

Indranil Ghosh

Publishers
Pustak Mahal®, **Delhi**

J-3/16 , Daryaganj, New Delhi-110002
☎ 23276539, 23272783, 23272784 • *Fax:* 011-23260518
E-mail: info@pustakmahal.com • *Website:* www.pustakmahal.com

Sales Centre
10-B, Netaji Subhash Marg, Daryaganj, New Delhi-110002
☎ 23268292, 23268293, 23279900 • *Fax:* 011-23280567
E-mail: rapidexdelhi@indiatimes.com

Branch Offices
Bangalore: ☎ 22234025
E-mail: pmblr@sancharnet.in • pustak@sancharnet.in
Mumbai: ☎ 22010941
E-mail: rapidex@bom5.vsnl.net.in
Patna: ☎ 3294193 • *Telefax:* 0612-2302719
E-mail: rapidexptn@rediffmail.com
Hyderabad: *Telefax:* 040-24737290
E-mail: pustakmahalhyd@yahoo.co.in

ISBN 978-81-223-0953-9

Edition : 2011

Printed at : Param Offsetters, Okhla, New Delhi-110020

Foreword

Feel good factors of life and the journey to success have a close and interdependent relationship. A strong desire to succeed can make life miserable provided enough care is not taken to make life enjoyable.

The path to success is always thorny. Many obstacles need to be overcome during its journey. Failures are bound to happen. In fact, according to Boris Pasternak – "In life, it is more necessary to lose than to gain. A seed will only germinate if it dies."

Failure alters our mood. We feel bad. However, we need to remain cheerful in such crucial moments too, keeping in mind that the true winners keep trying even when the going gets tough. An unfavourable frame of mind, rather 'Feel Bad' syndrome, is the biggest retardant to progress. It delays, even stops, the chances of success. Therefore, it is important to remain cheerful and 'Feel Good' even during adverse moments of life. In short, happiness must not fade away even during the days of struggles.

How it all started

Once, I met a college guy at a party. His T-shirt read – *'I feel better when I drink'*. There are millions of people worldwide who feel better by washing down their sufferings with a peg or two, or blowing out puffs of smoke. But is it the right way? Even if 'yes', is it long-lasting? Gradually, I started observing various other happy persons. I read a number of books on the subject. Informal interactions took place with many. Based on divergent experiences and vicarious learning of many HR experts, I carried out a few experiments on my own as well as others' lives.

One more incident took place almost at the same time. I had asked a young man – "Where can you find happiness?" His prompt reply was – "In discos!" His reply tempted me to visit a famous discotheque of the locality with one of my friends one evening. The rhythmic effect of song, dance, music already had our minds flying. It was indeed a nice feeling. Both of us observed the dancing crowd for a long time from one isolated corner of the room. Music stopped for a while, may be for changing the discs. Suddenly my friend asked me – "Can you tell me Indranil, what is the difference between pop songs and classical music?" No reply could immediately come out of my mouth. Soon the music started. The jazzy music and the youthful exotica of the crowd benumbed my thinking.

A few days later, my friend took me to a classical music concert. The first 30 to 40 minutes were really boring and monotonous. Gradually, I could feel the essence of the music and its soothing effect. It was making me feel better and better. My accompanying friend replied – "This is the difference. Pop songs compel your *body* to dance whereas your *mind* dances with classical music. As a result, your sorrows are healed, your mood is uplifted and you feel better. Later, I read a few articles on music therapy. How alpha waves of music soothe ill feelings and recharge the mind with positiveness is worth knowing.

All of us wish to live with prosperity and happiness. However, good times and bad times come in cyclic order. For bad times we never forget to blame the Devil and during good times, the same, we are forgetful to thank God.

To feel good and to remain good throughout is a state of mind. Remaining cool in adverse situations is the *mantra* for happiness or remaining good. 'Feeling Good' and 'Becoming Happy' are one and the same things. 'Feeling Better' is beyond that and I believe that it can be achieved easily by the use of certain methods.

Based on my practical observations, I tried to analyse and systematise the feel good factors of life. These feel good factors, after a lot of introspection, gave birth of ten various ways, whose regular practice will make a person feel better and better.

The book market is flooded with varieties of stuff, which prescribe people to always think positively to feel good. Remaining always positive is indeed the most difficult task. After all we are human beings. Anger, fear, jealousy and other negative emotions act as deterrents in the path of positive thinking. People are always in quest of simplified techniques. Therefore, my attempt here is not only to remain good but also to feel even better, and that too with very understandable methods.

When I had just started writing the book, my journalist friend Shamshed triggered a meaningful controversy in my mind by posing a question – "Are you sure that you feel and remain good always? If I ask your family members and close friends, will they have such an opinion about you? If in both the cases your answer is affirmative, only then you should go ahead, otherwise not." Shamshed's comments sowed a new seed of thought in my mind, which resulted in a fresh process of introspection. I thought more deeply and compared my present with my past, two years ago. My inner voice replied – "Yes! The time has ripened now to share my experiences with others."

The book is the outcome of all these. A blend of experimented theory and behavioural observance! Enough material is included in the book, which can additionally be used as a guide to success.

As Benjamin Franklin said – "Tell me and I forget; Teach me and I may remember; involve me and I learn." In various chapters of the book, I have recommended a few exercises. All of them are proven. Practise them repeatedly and get involved in the feel good process to achieve results fast.

The language used in this book has been kept as simple as possible. The approach is down to earth. Because of this anyone, irrespective of the individual's educational qualification, race, religion, cultural and social background, can use this book. Tide lifts all the boats. Let the tide of the book lift all to the world of 'living better.'

The Concept

Let us try to understand what 'feeling good' means. 'Feeling good' and 'feeling happy' are basically the same things. However, defining happiness as "a good feeling", we must keep in mind that 'good' is defined as being "something which causes happiness."

Once upon a time, there lived an aged man who was always seen cheerful and happy. All the people around him were surprised as to how this man could be happy when they themselves were unhappy facing innumerable problems. One day they asked the aged man – "How is that you are always happy and cheerful? You must be having a wonderful secret!" The old man said – "I don't have any secret. Every morning when I get up I have two choices; either to be happy or to be unhappy. I just choose to be happy." The aged man had in fact unfolded the very philosophy of happiness. What is happiness? Happiness is the state of one's mind.

In lay man's language, happiness represents good luck, good fortune, prosperity, etc. The dictionary meaning of happiness is an agreeable feeling or condition of the soul arising from good fortune or propitious happening of any kind; the possession of those circumstances or that state of being which is attended with enjoyment; the state of being happy; contentment; joyful satisfaction; felicity; blessedness.

We must agree that happiness is generic, and is applied to almost every kind of enjoyment. Its overlapping states or experiences include joy, exultation, delight, bliss, and love.

Happiness, rather components of *'Feel Good Factors'* can come from –

- ✦ **Past:** feelings of satisfaction, contentment, pride, and serenity.
- ✦ **Present** (examples): enjoying the taste of food, glee at listening to music, absorption in reading, and company of people you like, e.g., friends and family.
- ✦ **Future:** feelings of optimism, hope, trust, faith, and confidence.

Therefore, it can be said that 'Feel Good Factors' can be found with the remembrance of the past, activities of the present and our actions towards the future.

Happiness cannot be measured. It is an individual's personal feeling or an experience. It has no logical basis. A sadist may feel good by killing a person whereas a saint may feel good by saving a person.

➢ Pleasure and Happiness:

The term *pleasure* is sometimes used to indicate a short-term response, while *happiness* is sometimes used to refer specifically to a more long-term state. Historically, happiness was often thought of as success in life, including other things than how one feels. People also visualised success in one's plans, career, or social standing as happiness. Nowadays, terms such as *well-being* or *quality of life* are more often used and *happiness* is used for the felt experience or experiences that philosophers usually called *pleasure.*

Smoking, drinking, sex, etc., give pleasure not happiness. With smoking and drinking, pleasure soon turns into sorrow. However, sex, instead of a pleasure game may be looked upon as an instrument for improvement in relationship with spouse that leads to happiness.

Similarly enjoyment, relishing etc. give pleasure and not happiness.

➢ Comfort and Happiness:

Comfort and *Happiness* are not the same. *Happiness* is a state of mind but *comfort* is at the physical level. Often we mix up comfort and happiness. A person can still remain unhappy even if he/she is showered with all the comforts of the life. In the same way, a person in the most uncomfortable position also can remain happy. Let us take some imaginary case studies to understand it better.

First, think of two typical persons who live in any metropolitan city. Say, for example Harishbhai and Rajaram, both residents of the suburbs of Mumbai.

Harishbhai has a small fast-food stall in the Fort area. Office-goers of that area are his customers. His day starts at 8 am before the opening of offices and closes at 8 pm after the closure of those offices. He stays in Dombivili, a distant suburb of the city In the morning, he needs to walk 15 minutes to reach the station. Every morning, he leaves home with an aim to catch the 7.15 fast local to Mumbai CST, by which he is able to reach his workplace on time. He considers himself highly successful if he is able to reach the station a little early and catch the previous double-fast local. If he is not able to reach station on time, he has to lose his morning business as the next fast train is after a long interval and the slow train takes much longer. Often he wonders why whenever he reaches on time, that day the train is invariably late, and whenever he is late, the train leaves the platform on time! He is pleased if he is able to get inside the train. He considers himself very lucky if he gets a seat to sit. In between his 8 to 8 lifestyle, he has no room for anything else. In spite of all this, Harishbhai is happy.

He has a wife and two children. Every Sunday, he keeps his shop closed, visits the nearby temple in the early morning, spends the rest of the day with his family by including a trip to a fair, picnic or watching movies, eating out or any other entertaining activity. The relationship among his family members is very cordial. Children too understand their parents' difficulties and help them with the household chores. Signs of happiness can be seen on the faces of all his family members.

Another person, Rajaram, who stays in Thane, is a clerk in a government office. He loves to do things at leisure. He can do nothing fast enough. From his residential quarters, his office is hardly a few metres away. He does not like walking, as he feels that it is not a dignified way of maintaining lifestyle. He goes to office by auto-rickshaw. He gets up late. If he is late in office, he always has an excuse and proudly expresses it. He can be made to work only through bribes and gifts. He thinks it justifies and commensurates with his position and status. He fights daily with his wife and scolds the children without any significant reason. His children are non-cooperative. They have their own lifestyles. The entire family hardly passes the day together. His favourite time-pass for a holiday is sitting with a bottle of alcohol. He believes that 'a few pegs in the evening' is the secret of his happy living and others are jealous of his happiness. Whenever, he exceeds his limit, a spate of vulgar words flows out. The truth is, he is always unhappy although he always denies it.

The difference between these two persons – Harishbhai and Rajaram – is at their mental level. Both claim that they are happy. In the first case, happiness can be felt by others but in the latter case, happiness cannot be seen in the family.

In difficult times, positive thinking often brings happiness. We should know which one is actually positive thinking and which one is not.

Let us examine this example:

Mr. T. K. Das used to work as a supervisor in a big engineering firm. Due to various reasons, his performance fell. The management of the company issued him a warning. He felt insulted. He approached the court for justice. Hearing of the court went on for a long time. In the meantime, his relation with the company management spoiled further. Finally, he was fired. Because of all this, Mr. Das came under heavy financial crunch. It became impossible for him to bear legal expenses any more. He decided to discontinue the legal battle and withdrew his case. At present, he is sick, penniless – almost totally ruined both physically and mentally. But, if you meet him, you will always find false smiles on his face and a big claim of happiness. He still hopes that he will get justice one day. He strongly feels that the company's management will understand his problem and call him back to the job. Do you call this positive thinking?

➢ A Mexican story:

Let us understand the topic with one more story where the irony of the rat race is explained. This story is probably known to all of us through the blessings of the Internet.

A boat docked in a tiny Mexican village. An American tourist complimented the Mexican fisherman on the quality of his fish and asked how long it took him to catch them.

"Not very long," answered the Mexican.

"But then, why didn't you stay out longer and catch more?" asked the American.

The Mexican explained that his small catch was sufficient to meet his needs and those of his family.

The American asked, "But what do you do with the rest of your time?"

"I sleep late, fish a little, play with my children, and take a siesta with my wife. In the evenings, I go into the village to see my

friends, have a few drinks, play the guitar, and sing a few songs...I have a full life."

The American interrupted:

"I have an MBA from Harvard and I can help you. You should start by fishing longer every day. You can then sell the extra fish you catch. With the extra revenue, you can buy a bigger boat. With the extra money the larger boat will bring in, you can buy a second one and a third one and so on until you have an entire fleet of trawlers. Instead of selling your fish to a middleman, you can negotiate directly with the processing plants and maybe even open your own plant. You can then leave this little village and move to Mexico City, Los Angeles, or even New York City! From there you can direct your huge enterprise."

"How long would that take?" asked the Mexican.

"Twenty, perhaps twenty-five years," replied the American.

"And after that?"

"Afterwards? That's when it gets really interesting," answered the American, laughing. "When your business gets really big, you can start selling stocks and make millions!"

"Millions? Really? And after that?"

"After that you'll be able to retire, live in a tiny village near the coast, sleep late, play with your children, catch a few fish, take a siesta, and spend your evenings drinking and enjoying your friends!"

"I'm doing so now! Why should I do all that you suggested?" the Mexican replied.

Is the Mexican in the story really happy? Of course not! The fact is – man longs for happiness but happiness comes only from meaningful work.

The story may be projecting an unrealistic picture of happiness. The happiness that the Mexican is expressing is not the real one and its effect cannot be long-lasting. Basically, the person is lazy and his vision is choked. Soon, when he finds his peers overtaking him, he will become frustrated and land in the vicious cycle of negativity. In this context, we shall remember the famous saying of Benjamin Franklin – "Laziness travels so slowly that poverty soon overtakes him."

Try to understand the difference in the mental levels of Harishbhai, Rajaram, T.K. Das and the Mexican. All claim that they are happy. However, difference exists in their respective perceptions of happiness.

Therefore, it can be said that although happiness is individual perception, yet real happiness is always holistic. 'Feel Good Factors' should always aim towards real happiness, thereby not only making us happy but also transforming others who come across. Probably that is why someone said – "Happiness is a perfume which you cannot pour on others unless you have some on you."

Out of these four characters discussed above, only Harishbhai seems to be a really happy person in spite of all the adversities. His lifestyle is balanced. His happiness is to some extent holistic, as it conduced through the members his family. In other words – happiness is never perfect unless it is shared.

Contents

"Ten Commandments of feeling good"

'Feel Good' is characterised or designed to encourage a feeling of happiness or satisfaction. 'Feel Good Factors' or the activities which makes us 'happy' can be anything. Some of them could be – intimate relations, socialising, prayers, worship, meditation, eating, exercising, watching TV, shopping, chatting on the Internet or telephone, surfing the Internet, housework, working, commuting, driving, etc. Interacting with partners like spouse, friends, children, parents, relatives, boss, subordinates, client, customer, peers or even being alone can make us happy.

My friend Sagar has a slightly different perception. He feels that real happiness comes only through satisfaction. So, for perpetual happiness, reaching 'Unique Satisfaction Point (USP) is necessary, which is highly individualistic. USP is different for different person. A person may feel the essence of happiness in petty things but others may not feel so.

Whatsoever it may be, one thing is common in both these perceptions that behind every happiness, there is at least one factor. These feel good factors or activities can be grouped in the following way:

- ✦ **Material:** money, business, property, food, clothes, drugs and medicines, etc.

- **Social:** freedom, peace, shopping, friends, dating, flirting, family, music, etc.
- **Emotional:** love, romance, sex, company, etc.
- **Spiritual:** religion, enlightenment, *tantra*, meditation, etc.
- **Physical:** sleeping, drinking, sports, etc.
- **Others:** hobbies, decoration, work, cinema, etc.

Although it is good to satisfy our natural desires for food and drink, pleasures often conceal painful consequences. Therefore, feel good factors must be perpetual, related to only 'positive activities' and must lead to bliss, cheerfulness, enjoyment, exhilaration, and light-heartedness.

"Ten Commandments of feeling good" is an effort towards all these. My sincere belief is that the 'Feel Good Factors' are as real or as probable as 'Ten Commandments'.

➢ Perpetual Feel Good Factors – the Ten Commandments:

Following are the ten commandments to feel good always–

1. **Feel Good Factor No. 1:**

   Fake before you actually make.

   You are what you think you are. If you think that you are happy, you will really be happy. It is following up of a simple principle – **"Imagine, Pretend, and Act".** Imagine your happiness, pretend as if you are happy and act like a happy person. Always assume that you are always better than fine. *Make a slogan that makes you happy and chant it continuously for some time.* Let the slogan become the simplest *mantra* for becoming better and better, day by day!

2. **Feel Good Factor No. 2:**
   Improve Relationships.

   Happiness comes from relationship improvement. This is simply because you feel good when you are surrounded by people who like you. Improve relation with Self, God, Family, Relatives, and Friends.

   Realise the value of love. Spread love but ensure that you are in the company of right people at the right occasion. Blind love is dangerous; do not become its prey. Wrong company, especially with whom you cannot adjust easily, may make your life miserable. Be selective in choosing friends but have friends as many in numbers as possible. Adopt the **3A and 3C formula** for relationship improvement explained later in the book. Take advantage of Master-mind alliance and remain happy always.

   Remembrance of magic moments and other happy moments of the past makes us feel good. Recall them often to make you happy. Learn from history but never live in the past.

   Do remember, life is always charming and not drab. Enjoy life with the strokes of love and warmth of friendship and continue to feel better and better.

3. **Feel Good Factor No. 3:**
   Enjoy you power for happiness.

   Powerful people can live happily and peacefully. None ever dares to disturb them. Power is available in various forms. We hardly recognise them. Recognise the various forms of power available in abundance and grab them. Become powerful for feeling good forever.

Emotions are power, as well as serve as a major obstacle while discharging power. Learn to control emotions and utilise unused power. Win over negative emotions like anger, fear, jealousy etc., which make you unhappy. An emotionally balanced person is always happy, untouched by success or failure.

People often show their joy with a *smile.* So smile, even if it is artificial, to alter your mood. Laugh a lot and use it as a therapy to feel better.

4. **Feel Good Factor No. 4:**

   Trust self and others.

   Belief is everything. Happiness lies in trusting self. Never believe in rumours and superstition. They pollute the mind by posing mental blocks, generating suspicion, bringing down the self-confidence. Selfish people generate rumours for self-gain. Superstition is a stumbling block to progress.

   Positive thoughts bring happiness.

5. **Feel Good Factor No. 5:**

   Work and enjoy.

   Work is necessary to fulfil our needs. You feel good whenever your needs are fulfilled. So, any work, even a repetitive one, can be mood altering and entertaining. The only requirement is to recognise the entertaining part of the work.

   Enjoy your work but always dream for a bright future of your work. Forgetting the past, living in the present, and thinking about the road ahead are the seeds of happiness.

You also must have a noble cause to feel good, a mission of your life and a vision as driver. Attain goals to feel better. Accomplishments, one after another, make a person happy. Planning for future is essential to remain happy.

Discovering of the 'joy of work' is easier with Vision, Mission and Planning for the future. Practice ***'Karma Yoga'***. Remain dutiful without expectation. Expect ingratitude.

6. Feel Good Factor No. 6:

Good habit confers good feeling.

Identify your bad habits and prepare action plans to counter them. Correct use of antidotes may be required for old and chronic bad habits.

Always ensure that you have already shed your bad habits and are continuously developing good habits. If you move about with people who read books, listen to tapes, attend seminars, there is a good chance that you will pick up good habits.

Our food habit has a direct relationship with our feel good syndrome. Research shows that our mood often depends upon the type of food we eat. Happy energetic foods promote the feeling of well-being by releasing feel good neurons.

7. Feel Good Factor No. 7:

Cleanliness is happiness.

Cleanliness alters your mood. It assures good health by providing better hygiene. Health is wealth. Healthy body and healthy mind are each other's complements. Both physical cleanliness and mental cleanliness is necessary.

Happiness comes easily through spiritualism. Your mind is always filled with positive and spiritual thoughts.

There is place for everything and everything in its place. Housekeeping is an integral part of cleanliness.

8. **Feel Good Factor No. 8:**

   Adaptation is happiness.

   Any change can bring happiness. However, adaptation of self with the change is necessary to enjoy the change.

   The ABA (Alignment, Balancing and Adaptation) Theory is an approach on this line. Aligning self with the vision, balancing the needs and adapting self with the changed situation brings happiness.

9. **Feel Good Factor No. 9:**

   Relaxation and leisure.

   You feel better when you are relaxed. Manage time and relax – is the golden *mantra* for happiness. Follow a suitable and easy time management technique so that you get ample time for relaxation.

   Leisure is best enjoyed after hard work. So avoiding work is never recommended. Practice meditation and other relaxation techniques.

   Sleep well and feel better. Adequate sleep is required for survival. But remember, only sleep cannot bring happiness.

10. **Feel Good Factor No. 10:**

    Discover 'self', the in-built happiness.

    Discovering self will give happiness because the real meaning of happiness is available in abundance within us. Identify the happy person who lives within you. Remain content with whatever you already have. Never become selfish because selfishness gives pain, sacrifice gives pleasure. Be always 'owner's pride'; never 'neighbour's envy'.

Observe **silence** occasionally to feel better. Enjoy the life within with the power of silence and the bliss of contemplation.

Never indulge in petty politics because they do not serve any good purpose. Counter politics with an iron hand because they may disturb your happiness.

In the proceeding chapters I will discuss all these factors in more detail. Please understand that I am an ordinary person; I cannot bring a radical change in one's life. But certainly, my writings and my continuous effort to implant positive energy to others' lives will never make anyone bored. This book is nothing but an attempt on these lines.

Feel Good Factor ☺ 1

Fake before you make

It is said – "Better a lie that heals than a truth that wounds." Feel good factor number one "Fake before you make" is based on this belief. You are what you think you are. If you think that you are happy, you will be really happy.

So, it is the easiest way to feel good. This example will make you to understand how simple it is.

In one personality development program, the facilitator asked the participants – "How are you?"

Almost all replied – "Fine!"

The facilitator was not satisfied with the answer. He advised the class to say loudly – "Fantastic!" Trust me, it was like instant tonic. With the aloud utterance of the word "Fantastic!" most of the participants started feeling better and not just fine.

I have also made this trick a part of my life. Whenever, anyone asks me "How are you?" I reply loudly: "Fantastic!" I get positive energy with its chanting. Since the adoption of this trick, I have never felt my life as drab. My advice to you all is to follow this simple principle of life. Basically, by uttering the word "Fantastic", you will be creating a new and positive mental image in your subconscious mind. After a while, this image will imprint itself in your mind and your self-image will start changing. And you will realise the creation of a new soul within you. This may be called as –

'Fake before you make' phenomenon. When you are not confident enough about yourself, just try to behave and act like a confident person and this will boost up your confidence level automatically.

Our age-old learning and the advice of the elders – "Never tell lies. It is a sin. It is ethical to speak the truth always" may not hold good all the time. Harmless lies or a false statement often helps in many ways. Confidence building, mood alteration are a few of them.

What the mind of a man can conceive, and believe, it can achieve. Conceive happiness, you will get it. 'Fake before you make' basically is a way to implant happiness in the mind. When implanted, it gets nourishment and gradually spreads all over the mind and thereby conditioning or tuning the mind for happiness.

➢ The steps:

It has three essential steps – "Imagine – Pretend – Act". Whenever you are not in a good mood, think of some imaginary happiness. No harm even in fantasising. Pretend as if you are happy. Act as a really happy person. Within a short span, you will indeed feel better.

To get good results, the following steps are to be followed:

1. Find out the factor that makes you unhappy most of the time. As for example, say it is a relationship problem with others.
2. Next step is to prepare a slogan out of the unhappy factor. The slogan must be brief, catchy and one that exactly addresses the issue. 'Be happy, be popular', 'good relations, live long', 'happy days are here again', 'I smile to smile' – are a few examples of such slogans.
3. Chant the slogan throughout the day and night whenever possible for the next few days; especially

before going to bed and immediately after getting up from sleep, and whenever you do not have anything special to do.

Chanting a *mantra* or *shloka* is an ancient tradition of our culture. Most of the religions advocate chanting, and illustrate it as one of the ways to reach God or get enlightenment. The only difference here is what we have to chant is a slogan.

The subconscious mind is as sensitive as an innocent child is. When you train a child, repetition is required. Repeated chanting will create a rosy picture in your mind. Then, your reality comes true before your expectation. Soon your relationship with others will improve and you will feel better and better.

Let us understand how 'fake before you make' actually acts. It is said that the mind is like wet cement, whatever falls on it makes an impression. Even if you fake, the mind will accept its impression.

➢ Positive affirmation:

Positive affirmation does this job of impression. One such simple but effective positive affirmation is given below. Follow the given steps:

1) Sit in a comfortable position with the backbone straight, heels touching each other.
2) Concentrate on your breathing.
3) Say in your mind – "Relax! Relax! Relax!"
4) Imagine and talk to yourself –

I. Today is going to be a great day.

II. I can handle more than I think I can.

III. I will be satisfied when I try to do my best.

IV. There is always something to be happy about.

V. I will make someone happy today.

VI. Every day in every way, I get better and better.

5) Continue to remain like this for some more time and enjoy the silence within.

If you practice this positive affirmation day after day, you will feel better and better.

➢ Sub-conscious, Conscious and Unconscious Mind:

I will not go into a detailed discussion on Sub-conscious, Conscious and Unconscious Mind. I will only highlight a few points. Conscious Mind is a wakeful state and Unconscious Mind is the sleeping state of mind. The peculiarity of the Subconscious mind is –

- ✦ It is always working from birth to death. Never goes off.
- ✦ It works from the background. It creates a prompting effect on the conscious mind.
- ✦ At a certain time it is activated. You yourself can activate it by going into meditation or deep relaxation.
- ✦ It does not understand logic. And does not recognise 'No' or 'Don't' instructions. Hence, while activating and programming it, only affirmative instructions are to be given.
- ✦ Sub-conscious and Conscious minds operate like a seesaw. In wakeful state, conscious mind is more prominent whereas in sleeping state, sub-conscious mind is vigilant. In meditative state, both sub-conscious and conscious minds are balanced.

A sick person, who has no apparent reason to feel happy, can not only really become happy through adoption of 'fake before you make' but can also expect an early recovery.

Feel Good Factor ☺ 2

Relationship improvement makes us happy

One of the most important feel good factors is healthy and improved relationship with self, God, family, friends and the society.

Happiness comes from relationship improvement simply because you feel good when you are surrounded by the people who like you. Harishbhai's family is happy because a healthy relationship exists among the members.

Various persons may adopt various methods for relationship development. But the most effective principle of such relationship betterment rests in the spreading of love. A few of the relationship betterment tools are:

- With self – meditation, relaxation, nurturing hobbies, etc.
- With God – daily prayer, worships, etc.
- With family and friends – greetings, birthday wishes, encouragement, avoiding fighting and arguments, etc.
- With society – voluntary and social work, donation, raising funds for a noble cause, etc.

Any 'Improvement' always starts with 'I'. So, relationship improvement must also start with 'self'. Most of the people feel that relation means any affiliation with others and that needs to be improved. The truth is without improving your relationship with yourself, you can not really achieve 'relationship improvement' upto its fullest extent.

Some people smoke for the sake of pleasure (difference between pleasure and happiness has already been explained). By smoking they abuse their body. There are many other ways of self-abuse like over or under eating, untimely sleeping, shying away from physical exercise, etc. If self-abuses are not discontinued, relationship with self cannot be improved. If the relationship with self is not good, the relationship with others may not remain good forever.

➢ Communication is the basis of effective relationship:

Where there is effective communication, harmony exists and relationship builds up. Free and honest communication builds up trust and relationship cannot build up without trust. Lack of free and open communication may generate mistrust, rumour, superstition, etc.

➢ Love and Friendship

You may be surprised that when a simple method like fake before you make is available for feeling good, then why I am also trying to put stress on love, friendship and many other things. Human beings are social entities. As good relationship is the major contributor for remaining good, a vivid knowledge on 'love and friendship' will be helpful to understand 'relationship management' in a better way.

Let us start with – what is love? There are many definitions, but this one I liked most. *"Expression of Love mathematically: With God as centre and love as radius, draw a circle of your life. In that life, add your friends. Subtract your enemies. Multiply your joys. Divide your sorrows and get happiness as a remainder."*

Love begets love. Sharing of love, both giving and taking, brings happiness. That is why it is said that love, not time, heals all wounds. Similarly when love becomes thin, faults appear thicker.

➢ Liking and Love

Can you tell me the difference between the two?

Both of them are feelings, emotional stages of life. Both sound similar, synonymous, yet they are different. You may like a person or an article but it does not necessarily mean that you love them.

If you are attracted to something or someone, it is 'liking'. But if you care for it and take its onus, it is your love for it. Mind it; I said 'onus' and not 'possess.' If you love someone, you must care for that person.

If you try to help someone during his/her difficult day, it is your sympathy. But, if your heart cries on listening someone's sorrow, and if the person's agony becomes yours then it is not sympathy, it is empathy. Liking someone empathetically is love. Mathematically, you can express it as–

"Love = Liking + Empathic Caring"

One negative thing that often gets attached with 'love' is 'emotional bursting,' often leading towards 'showing off.' When a person falls in love, he/she does not care for any rules or norms. The person simply wants to possess it immediately. Possessing of love may not happen instantly. So he/she tries to show him/her off. Even after possession, the false fear of losing the love makes the person afraid. Here, too, he/she tries to show off, even tell lies. Often complexity, either superior or inferior develops. Therefore, the foundation of love weakens and mistrust builds up. Anger, frustration, etc. creep in. The love shatters within no time, and the failure rate in love marriages is much more than in arranged ones.

Therefore, the lovers must know each other well, so that they learn to love each other empathetically.

➢ What is empathic love?

Swami Chinmayananda said -- "In life, to judge others use your heart and to judge yourself use your head." Empathy is the ability of a person to see from the other person's viewpoint. Even children can understand it. Here is a small but lovely story:

There lived a beautiful girl child Pinky with her parents. The real tough job for her parents was to feed her. One morning at the breakfast table the scene was usual – the mother nagging the daughter's apathy to milk. When the father asked his darling daughter: "Dear Pinky, why not a glass of milk for your dad's sake?"

Pinky thought for a while and replied – "Dad, if I drink the full glass, will you give me whatever I ask for?"

"Of course darling," was dad's reply.

Slowly and painfully, Pinky finished it all. The very next moment was the child's expectation. All attention was on her.

"Dad, I want to have my head shaved off?"

"What? A girl child wants to shave off her head! Impossible." Her mother blew off.

"Dad, you are going back on your words." The child cried.

"Okay! Promises must be kept. But every day you have to drink at least one glass of milk."

The father modified the terms and the daughter agreed to it without a second thought.

With head clean shaved Pinky went to school on that day. Her father dropped her at the school. Pinky waved, turned around and waved, her father too waved back with a smile. Just then a boy alighted from a nearby car and shouted, "Pinky, please wait for me." What struck the father was the hairless head of the boy.

"Sir, your daughter is great indeed." Without introducing herself, a lady got out of the car and continued, "That boy who is walking with your daughter is my son. He is suffering from cancer."

Soon it became clear why Pinky wanted to shave her head. The boy lost his hair due to the side-effects of chemotherapy. He refused to attend school fearing cruel teasing from his schoolmates. Pinky wanted to share the teasing with the boy. Probably this is called 'empathic love', the true meaning of friendship.

➢ Features of love:

An old proverb – "Wilds are beautiful in jungle and the babies in mothers' lap" is appropriate in case of love. Love is beautiful and continues to remain beautiful unless it is pampered. Once you try to possess love, its beauty gets spoilt.

Have you done window-shopping? How immense the temptations! Every time, you see an attractive and beautiful article, you feel like possessing it. But, once you buy it, your attraction towards it lessens. That is why many a times we find expensive household items like vacuum cleaner, VCD, etc. kept in one corner and treated with sheer negligence. Love is also like that. It is beautiful as attractive, so long as it is out of our reach.

Love is a behaviour and a feeling, certainly not an article. Hence, never can it be owned. Never try to snatch love. It is natural and cannot become anyone's property. So, never mix up love with self-interest or accomplishment. Blind love is dangerous; do not become its prey.

Often love is compared with a wineglass. If you hold it loose, it slips out of your palm. If you hold it too tight, it breaks, often injuring you. Like knowledge, love also ascends if shared.

It is often said – *"Giving leads to empathic love."* What is giving? True giving is other-oriented, and requires the following four elements:

- ✦ The first is care, demonstrating active concern for the recipient's life and growth.
- ✦ The second is responsibility, responding to his/her expressed/unexpressed need.
- ✦ The third is respect, the ability to see the other person as he/she is and be aware of his/her unique individuality.
- ✦ The fourth and most important is knowledge. You can care for, respond to, and respect the other only if you know him/her deeply.

The more you give, the more you love. That is why probably our parents, who have given us more than we ever know, undoubtedly love us more than we love them. And, in turn, we love our children more than they will love us. This is because deep and intimate love emanates from knowledge and giving; it comes not overnight but over time.

Where true love is present, happiness is bound to come. About **'True Love'** Swami Vivekananda in one of his writings had said:

"I would like to share something on the 'nature of love.' I once had a friend who grew to be very close to me. Once when we were sitting at the edge of a swimming pool, she filled the palm of her hand with a little water and held it before me, and said this: "You see this water carefully contained on my hand? It symbolises Love." This was how I saw it: "As long as you keep your hand carnally open and allow it to remain there, it will always be there. However, if you attempt to close your fingers around it and try to possess it, it will spill through the first cracks it finds."

This is the greatest mistake that people commit when they meet love, they try to possess it, they demand, they expect; and just like the water spilling out of your hand, love will run away from you. For love is meant to be free, you can not change its nature. If there are people you love, allow them to be free beings. Give and don't expect. Advise, but don't order. Ask, but never demand. It might sound simple, but it is a lesson that may take a lifetime to truly practice. It is the secret to true love. To truly practice it, you must sincerely feel no expectations from those who you love, and yet an unconditional caring."

Our life is a perfect reflection of our beliefs – "Some people make the world special just by being in it."

Love can be of various other types –

- ✦ Abstract – e.g., A mechanic loves his machine.
- ✦ Physical – e.g., The lovers love each other so much that they want to remain together.
- ✦ Sensual – Love comes out as a physical expression like kissing.
- ✦ Platonic love – It is an affectionate relationship into which the sexual element does not enter, especially in cases where one might easily assume otherwise.

One more type – Love at first sight – this puppy love is short-lived.

In a recent study in the US, it was found that romance in a relationship makes both men and women happier than those involved in a casual association. According to this study, romantic relationships, ranging from casual dating to marriage, have the potential to affect people's mental and physical health, sexuality and financial status.

Love lasts longer only when there is no mutual expectation. If at all expectations are present, they must be realistic.

➢ Lust – The bodily love:

Bodily love, though it sounds like a type of love, may have or may not have a love component in it. Lust is the genesis of such type of love.

Truly, lust is a desire and not love. However, a lovely feeling and relationship may develop later which may get transformed into love.

Lust is considered a vice by many religions. Some moralists consider lust to be a corruption of temperance, in the sense that when temperance fails, lust is the natural result. In Christian theology, it is considered one of the seven deadly sins.

Once, I had written an article on 'Woman, wine and war.' Through that article, I basically tried to correlate these three. When I visited Ms. Shamshed Ali Baig, a newspaper editor, with the article and got engrossed in a discussion, a completely different dimension of the topic opened up. According to her, it's the men's lust, which is the only reason for most of the crimes against women.

What is men's lust? Probably all of us understand. It's like hunger or fulfilment of desires. Is it not a necessary devil? Yes! It is. Then, why to blame the lust alone?

But always remember that love is clean but lust is not. Lust spoils the love. Hence, never mix the two.

➢ Magic moments:

We feel good with its remembrance. What is the real meaning of magic moments? These are the moment when we feel blessed and so happy that we cannot express our feelings in words, e.g. the magical moment when we first realise that we are in love. It can happen anywhere, at any time and under any circumstances whatever – but it is sheer magic and the memory remains with us all our lives.

Exercise:

Please write down when you fall in love with someone for the first time. How many similar occasions came in your life? How you felt on each occasion? Just think, don't you feel happy remembering them? Hunt out or generate similar moments with your spouse and bring back happier days in your life. If single, remember those magic moments and feel better and better.

➢ Friendship

Friendship is a type of interpersonal relationship. Making friends is as common as any other activity in our society. That is why probably a man is always eager to make friends. It is also said that a man is best judged by the company he keeps. Friends are the best reflection of your personality.

The main advantage of having friends is that you feel happy whenever you have company of a friend. Networking or building up a long list of friends and acquaintances is necessary for progress. It is said – "Have you fifty friends? It is no enough. Have you one enemy? It is too much."

Without friends, relatives and acquaintances you are lonely. Loneliness kills. Studies have proved it. Lonely people have blood pressure readings as much as 30 points higher than same age group non-lonely people. A lonely person become hostile and grows older at a faster rate.

Aristotle said: "What is a friend? A single soul in two bodies." Many people will walk in and out of your life. But only true friends will leave footprints in your heart. Spread love and realise its value but ensure that you are in the company of the right people at the right time. Wrong company, especially with whom you cannot adjust, may make your life miserable. Be selective in choosing friends but have friends in as many numbers as possible.

Your friends will stretch your vision or choke your dreams. Therefore, choose your friends very carefully – get rid of toxic people, who try to spread negative thinking. Never develop a friendship with a man who is not better than you.

Friends have a great influence on us. A good friend can become a guide, philosopher and an instrument for our success and happiness. Contrary to this, a bad friend can pull us down to hell within no time. Like true love, true friendship is also associated with faith and trust. A person whom you cannot trust or has failed to win over your confidence, is no way your friend.

You automatically feel good when you are in the company of good people and trustworthy friends. Hence, before you pick your friends, you must know which friend is appropriate for which occasion.

A proverb says – "An empty cattle shed is better than to have a herd of unruly cows!" Most of our friends who move around us are either opportunists or negative thinkers. Get rid of them. Always beware of freelance advisors.

➢ Varieties of friends:

There are various types of friends. Sometime or the other, we come across almost all of them. We cannot live without friends but choosing the right ones is always in our hands. Natures and types of friends are discussed below:

❖ *Happy time friends or friendship for pleasures or time-pass friendship:*

They are also known as friendship for pleasure – casual friendship. Such friends show signs of intimacy only when there is no internal or external disturbance. Hence, such friendship is very short-lived. Even a minor disarrangement may mean the end of the friendship. Always beware of such friends!

❖ *Crisis time friends or friendship for the survival:*

Such friends show unusual signs of friendship when the friends (or group members) work under pressure like approaching of the target date at workplace, industrial disputes, riots, etc., or during emergency, fire-fighting type of jobs, etc. Such friendships are also short-lived but welcome. Friendships are lost once the crisis is over. Some people opine that good and useful friends are those who show their friendship during times of crisis.

❖ *Friendship for achievement*

Motivated employees at workplaces try to satisfy their higher order needs. They want to achieve something, which is distinct, rare and praiseworthy. This motivational force keeps the members united Such type of friendship can be found during group events of sports like football, hockey, etc. This type of friendship is also known as friendship for benefit.

❖ *Total friendship or real friendship or all-time friendship:*

Here, the friends always remain united irrespective of any inter or external happenings. The friends are tightly bonded with each other socially and emotionally and always tend to remain loyal to each other. The past performances and deeds of the each and every friend plays a significant role to build up the loyalty, which becomes a matter of pride for them and hence, continue to keep the friendship intact.

Another type of friendship also can be seen, which is friendship for principles. Like-minded people flock together. Though all four types of friendship as mentioned above can be seen here, yet real friendship can also be easily found here.

There are two other classifications also:

- **Reliable** and
- **Unreliable**

The friends, whom you cannot rely upon, are not at all friends. It is better to have enemies than unreliable friends.

Friendship during happy periods is very common. Friendship during crisis time is also not very rare. Friendship for achievement is basically opportunity-based friendship, which is a state of friendship where the entire group is highly motivated and becomes united to accomplish its desire of reaching the goal. This type of unity can be achieved through healthy competition, motivation, able leadership, clear-cut policy, well-defined objective, etc. This type of unity is most wanted by business, industrial houses and also for political achievements. Such type of unity, though rare, but is possible to obtain.

Total friendship is rarely noticed. Such friends are always reliable. Yet, this is also one of the most wanted forms of unity. This type of friendship reflects the real meaning of friendship, which can ideally be seen everywhere, from the *Raj-darbar* to the "burning ghat" and during festivals and revolutions in the country. Total friendship almost never breaks because of its inbuilt loyalty. Therefore, it is the most valued form of friendship.

➢ Pen friend or e-friendship:

Friendship or love of the new generation! Is this really friendship? Debatable! Nowadays, we come across stories about e-mail friendship, Net friendship and marriages through them. These raise a fundamental doubt. Can two persons become and remain friends without actually meeting each other? However, networking is possible through such friendship.

➢ How to choose a friend?

There is an old saying in Sanskrit : *Rajadware smashane, rashtrabiplabe sa ja tishthati sa bandhava.* (the person who is always with you in the king's court, burning place, during revolution is friend").

Before taking an appropriate decision, let us understand the various types of friends. Choosing the right ones is no doubt difficult. It needs a very careful watch. If you do not find a real friend, at least try and look for a reliable one.

➢ How to maintain friendship?

Making friendship is easy but maintaining it forever is the most difficult job. Good friendship is the result of good relationship development. For long-lasting friendship, one needs to do the following:

- ✦ Know your friend. The more you know your friend, the easier it will be for you to deal with him/her. There is always something to learn from each and every person.

- ✦ Use relationship development formula – 3A and 3C.

❑ ***3A – Accept, Adjust, Appreciate:***

- Accept your friend as whatever he or she is. Do not become his/her teacher.
- Try your best to adjust yourself wherever you are.
- Always appreciate genuinely the good side of your friend and stand firmly behind him or her for a noble cause.

❑ ***3C – Condemn, Criticise, Complain:***

- Never condemn your friend but educate him/her. Show with examples.
- Implant positive energy in him.
- Show him/her a way out; guide in such a way that within a short span he/she can raise his/her head proudly.

- Honestly appreciate him. Never criticise him/her in public. If at all criticism is necessary, do it in privacy.
- Never complain about your friend. If she/he makes a mistake, correct him.

✦ Out of sight, out of mind. Remember your friend's birthday, anniversary, festivals he/she celebrates and never forget to wish on these occasions. Occasionally, remember your friend by sending flowers, e-mails, telephone calls, etc.

✦ Show your friendship. Help him/her whenever he/she is in distress. But always remain mentally prepared to accept ingratitude.

➢ Dale Carnegie's golden principles of relation improvement:

Dale Carnegie, as young man, was a failure. As a student he was never popular. He tried to become a salesman; everyone rejected him. He felt like committing suicide. Suddenly, he thought that as it is he had wasted his life, then why not try to find out how there were so many successful people around. He started interviewing people and finally came to the conclusion that all successful people had one thing in common and that was their wonderful relationship with the people around them. Dale Carnegie came out with the golden principles of human relation improvement. Some of these golden principles are:

✦ **Do not criticise, condemn or complain:** This we have already discussed as 3C formula. The basis of this principle is – if we ask a hundred people whether they would like to be criticised, all of them would probably say 'No.' If we do not like criticism, everybody else will also not like it. Hence, stop criticising, condemning and complaining, because they spoil relations.

- **Show honest and sincere appreciation:** This is different from flattery. Flattery comes from lips but honest and sincere appreciation comes from the heart.
- **Arouse in the other person an eager want** to improve in his own life, and he falls in love with you. This is a little difficult to understand. In those days my posting was at a remote place. Once, a gentleman had come to visit our site. When we were in conversation, Nagappa the attendant was curiously listening to us. After the person had left, I asked Nagappa what he had understood from our conversation. Nagappa sadly replied: "Nothing, as I do not know English." I asked him whether he wished to speak like us. He showed his zeal with a great smile. I taught him a few words of simple English. Since then, Nagappa has become my friend.
- **Smile:** We have already discussed that by smiling we do not become poor but we enrich the lives of other people. In China, there is a proverb – "If you do not have a smiling face, you cannot become a shopkeeper."
- **Name:** Remember people's names and they will be obliged to you.
- **Be a good listener:** Encourage others to talk about themselves.
- **Talk in terms of the other man's interest**: The *Vashi Times*, the oldest English news weekly of Navi Mumbai, generally publishes local news and other news-related articles. Once, it broke all of its traditions and published one of my fictions. What was so special about my fiction? Nothing special, but when I met the editor with my fiction, I had talked only about the improvement of their newspaper and explained how the story could be a new attraction. And it was enough to get my work published.

- ✦ **Make the other person feel important** and do it very sincerely. The equation is very simple – the higher you go, the more is the courtesy; the more is the courtesy, the higher you go.

➢ Friendship & partnership:

My friend, Palash often says – 'ship' is a dicey word. It's not difficult to have one but hard to maintain. Even when it adds up with some other word to make a different meaning, then too its characteristics never change. My friend means the terms 'friendship', partnership' etc. contain the word 'ship' and have similar characteristics.

We know it's difficult, yet we venture all these 'ships' often out of compulsion. Therefore, we need to assure certain safeguards to bond better.

In partnership, two or more persons are involved, often by choice but mostly out of compulsion or with specific purpose. Partnership, in whatever form it may be such as lab-partner, room partner, business partner, etc, is the laboratory of friendship.

➢ Partnership in business:

The other day, I was talking to my old businessman-friend Samaddar. We discussed various aspects of business including partnership in business. Many important apprehensions were revealed. Let me point out his advice in a structured way. These have to be kept in mind before venturing out on a partnership business:

- ✦ Do not start a partnership business of which you do not have sufficient knowledge or you will be mostly depending on your partner's lore.
- ✦ Yet, if you try to initiate such a business, keep a strict tab on day-to-day activities. Any suspicion should prompt you to rethink about your involvement.

- ✦ Avoid partnership unless it is absolutely essential.
- ✦ Always remain alert. Trust must not generate overnight. Remain watchful even of your trusted buddies.
- ✦ Become professional with your partners in business activities.
- ✦ Never mix up business with your personal and family life.

Partnership may be inevitable due to various reasons. However, from day one, care should be taken so that it gives happiness always and never turns into hostility. The tips Mr. Samaddar gave to me were based on his own perception. To me, the last two points 'to remain professional' and 'not to mix up professional relationship with personal' are most important. However, no relation can really build up without trust. Partnership is no exception.

➢ Marriage, the biggest partnership:

Arranged or Love marriage?

In love marriage, the partner is a known person. Both good and bad habits, likings, weaknesses are known. Post-marriage adjustments are supposed to be less.

But most of the time, the person falls in love because of some strong appealing factor and the positive sides of the partner. The negative points surface only after marriage, and create problems. However, often the partners spend a lot of time with each other. This creates better understanding between the two, that helps later on.

On the contrary, in arranged marriage, the partners do not know each other. Partners are chosen through rich experiences of the parents/guardians, who are generally in a position to take a better decision.

➢ Right company:

Once upon a time there lived a beetle and a bumblebee. They were very good friends. The bumblebee used to hang around the lotus pond to savour nectar from lotus flowers. Cow-dung was the beetle's favourite cuisine and he did not know the taste of lotus. One day, the bumblebee invited the beetle to the lotus pond to taste lotus at least once. The beetle accepted the invitation.

For the beetle, it was a unique experience. He was really delighted to move from one lotus to another and suck its nectar. At the end of the day, when it was the time to return, the bumblebee called him back. But, he remained so blissful that he told the bumblebee to go back alone, as he would return later. So, the bumblebee had to return alone. A short while later, the beetle felt tired and slept over one of the lotus flowers. The petals of lotus usually close at night. Here, too, the same thing happened and the beetle got trapped inside the flower. The hapless beetle shouted for help but in vain. He then had only one option left, to wait for the sunrise.

The king of that country was a pious man. He used to worship his deity with a lotus every morning. At dawn, the king came to take a bath in the pond, plucked the lotus in which the beetle was trapped, carried it on his head to his palace temple and offered the flower at the feet of his deity. By then it had become morning. Along with the sunrise, the petals of the lotus started opening out and within a few moments the beetle was free. The beetle was now happier because he had just had the opportunity to be on the head of the king and the feet of God. He thanked the bumblebee for taking him to the lotus pond.

Moral: Right company may change your destiny. Hence always choose right company.

Once I met a 65-year-old retired person, Raghunath. He said: "I always make friendship with the people who are younger than me in age." Persons like Raghunath claim that mingling with younger people makes them feel young. My friend Vimal loves to have friendship with women. This is not flirting. The company of the fairer sex makes him feel good. Like Raghunath and Vimal, all of us have choices and preferences to choose friends. We also have special persons in our life, whose presence makes us happy. Right company is an important feel good factor for us.

➢ MasterMind Alliance – platform to choose right company:

"A MasterMind Alliance," as defined by Napoleon Hill, "is the coordination of knowledge and effort, <u>in a spirit of harmony</u>, between two or more people, for the attainment of a definite purpose." The fundamental concept of MasterMind alliance is the power of collective thinking. Why does one need to join a MasterMind alliance? Because, it is better for people to do something and pay nothing, than to pay dues and do nothing.

Immediately after attending a personality development program, all of us were enthusiastic. But the facilitator had cautioned that the tempo the workshop gave mostly cools down after some time unless we are careful. We never wanted our spirits to slow down. We were excited to create a platform, through which we could share our experiences and knowledge and re-brush ourselves; ultimately that would keep us always positively charged. And that was the genesis of our "Winners' Club", which was nothing but a meeting place for a group of people like us, who believe in happy living and winning in life throughout. There, we compulsorily used to take part in public speaking sessions. We used to speak about the benefits obtained by us by remaining positive. We used to discuss about our experiences on the various adversities of life, which could be overturned through positive mental attitude. We also used to deliver talks on different topics. Trust me, the results were astonishing.

MasterMind alliance creates the right atmosphere. It is a great source of power. It brings like-minded, achievement-oriented individuals together in one place to leverage each other's success. You can become happy by tapping power from it.

Right environment is required for happy living. Think of the Bihari labourers. In Bihar, they give low output but the same labourers in Punjab are highly productive. Similarly, in Kerala, Keralite workers are always busy with tantrums of trade unionism. That is why there are fewer industries in Kerala. However, Keralite workmen are often preferred in Mumbai and the Gulf countries.

In both cases the reason is common – environment. It is the environment that increases the output of the people. Shiv Khera has said: "In a positive environment, a marginal performer's output goes up. In a negative environment, a good performer's output goes down. MasterMind alliance creates such positive environment around us."

➢ Networking:

Networking is simply increasing the circle of your friends and known persons so that a bigger number of referrals is available to you. It is one of the easiest ways to net a success. It is a simple process of forming, discovering and utilising connections between the people, and is based on the theory– 'the more number of people you know, the more is your chance to become successful'. Like it or not, this relatively old-fashioned tool is used effectively by all successful people. If you are in search of a job or wish to fix up an alliance for your daughter, or simply want to increase your business volume, networking will come to your rescue.

➢ The learning:

Do remember, life is always charming and not drab. So, enjoy life with the strokes of love and warmth of friendship and continue to feel better and better.

Feel Good Factor ☺ 3

Happy people are the powerful people

Become powerful for feeling good forever. Learn to control emotions, gain power and utilise unused power.

Ancient Hindu and Buddhist philosophy says that the man has within him all the power required for overcoming his difficulties and problems. However, it is necessary to build a superior mind that gives greater strength and ability to fulfil the desire and ensure a happy living.

Power is available in various forms. We hardly recognise them. If at all we recognise, we often fail to reach them out.

My former boss often used to say about problems – they are like time bombs. One does not know when they will burst. Two options are available to you to save yourself from their devastation. Either you defuse it or pass it to others. The best is to defuse – either by self or by seeking help from others. The powerful people can do both, based on situations and hence, are most unlikely to damage themselves through its action.

We feel better when we are powerful. So, be powerful to feel better. The corridor of power is always crowded with power-hungry people. To them power means money power, manpower, muscle power, etc. In short, power of a position. We often come across political leaders who are proud of their 'power of positions' and the money and muscle power they use to tackle any awkward situation and turn the tables on their side.

But this is not the only form of power. A saint or a true leader, without the use of such power, can convince people and pull a larger crowd to their side. So, there are many other forms of power, which are very effective to get success and happiness. Unfortunately, for grabbing them there is no competition, yet we are not enthusiastic to capture them.

Some of these powers are:

- ✦ Power of emotion
- ✦ Power of asking
- ✦ Mind power and willpower
- ✦ Power of thinking
- ✦ Power of believing
- ✦ Power of knowledge
- ✦ Power of convincing
- ✦ Power of silence
- ✦ etc., etc., etc. ...

There can be very long list. However, the sum and substance is that no one really needs to wait for a position to grab power. Anyone can become powerful by picking a few from the list of powers readily available.

Power can be real as well as imaginary. Even an imaginary power confers a sense of happiness. What is an imaginary power? This could be a right example:

In rural areas, especially where caravans pass, readers might have seen often a bullock cart is pulled by a pair of oxen with a dog tied to a rope in the space between the oxen. If one of the bullocks slows down or tries to graze, the dog barks. The bullocks immediately speed up. This makes the dog happy because it gives a false feeling of power to the dog, which feels that it is not only pulling the cart but controlling the movement of the bullocks as well.

Out of the long list of power, I will discuss a few of them to make you understand that acquiring power is not at all difficult.

1.0 Power of Emotions:

Strongest of all the powers mentioned above is the power of emotion. Emotions are of two types – Positive and Negative. Love, courage, joy, enthusiasm, etc. are positive emotions. People often show their joy with a *smile.* Smile is nothing but an expression of positive emotions. Anger, hate, fear, worry, etc. are negative emotions. Similarly restlessness, crying, shirking etc. are the expression of negative emotions.

Laugh is a louder expression of smile. Laugh can be used as therapy to cure diseases, altering mood and bringing overall happiness. It is said that Norman Cousins, editor of the *Saturday Review* for 35 years was diagnosed with a painful and progressively degenerative disease. He was told that he did not have long to live. Mr. Cousins left the hospital and watched a lot of comedy shows. He slowly recovered fully and returned to work. Later, after 15 years, he suffered a heart attack. That time too, an overdose of laughter sailed him through. He narrated his experience in *The Healing Heart.*

Positive emotions bring happiness. Negative emotions bring unhappiness. However, positive emotions need not always be good; there is a good side of negative emotions and a bad side of positive emotions also. But generally, winning over negative emotions like anger, fear, jealousy etc. can make us happy.

"A ship in harbour is safe. But that is not what ships are built for." We are like a ship or an airplane where our mind is the pilot and emotions are its fuel. Emotions are a very powerful fuel. Influenced by emotions, we are able to do unusual things. We can perform both heroic and barbaric acts. This is another way of looking into this. So only winning over our negative emotions will not help always. We have to learn the balanced use of emotions. Emotionally balanced persons use their emotions in a controlled manner. They are untouched by success or failure and they are always very happy.

Emotions force us to do any of the following:

- **Decision** – life changing decisions. Often wrong decisions are taken. We become unhappy.
- **Disgust** – it is like 'enough is enough' and we quit. We lose patience and persistence. As a result we lose.
- **Desire** – e.g. 'I want it now.' Supports willpower and generates enthusiasm.
- **Resolve** – what does it mean? Verb of resolution – New Year resolution – promising yourself. Corrective measures are taken to improve further.

All the actions we take based on emotions can be good as well as bad. So, proper management of emotions is necessary. Always remember the following:

- Most of the time we make our decisions based on emotions.
- Decisions taken on the basis of unmanaged emotions are disastrous.
- Make your emotions work for you and certainly not against you.

Among decision, disgust, desire and resolve, emotional decision is most critical. We must discuss it in elaboration.

➢ Emotional decisions:

Often decisions or actions are taken based on emotions. These often invite unhappiness. A few days ago, a send off function was arranged for one of our good friends, who hopped to another organisation. During the farewell speech, one of my colleagues expressed whether our friend had taken an emotional decision, which might not be an appropriate one. Such doubts are genuine because one of the important factors that influence our decisions is emotion.

All of us are the slaves of our emotions. It is said our progress or success in life depends on the way we manage our emotions. A success depends upon only 20% IQ but 80% EQ. Therefore, it is very important to know about emotions so as to achieve full control over it. Our life will change if we add intelligence to emotions. Through the development of emotional intelligence, we can develop good emotional habits.

Let us do a small exercise to understand it better. Close your eyes. Imagine that you are blind. Can you see anything? Yeah! You can see a lot. You can see through mind as well as heart. What our hearts can see, our eyes cannot. Whatever we see through our eyes is all real not imaginary. But what heart and mind see can be both real and imaginary; this is called emotional viewing. Practice emotional viewing regularly to understand the difference between real and imaginary objects. Then take a decision.

➢ Emotional malaise or emotional disease:

Prolonged exposures to uncontrolled emotions result in emotional diseases. Symptoms of these diseases are –

- ✦ Withdrawal or social problems: preferring to be alone, lacking energy, feeling unhappy, being overly dependent, etc.
- ✦ Anxious and depressed: being lonely; having many fears and worries; needing to be perfect; feeling nervous or depressed.
- ✦ Attention or thinking problem: unable to pay attention or sit still, daydreaming, acting without thinking, unable to get mind off thoughts.

- ✦ Delinquent or aggressive: lying and cheating (preferably with children), arguing a lot, demanding attention (like me), destroying other things (example burning down hospital),

Like any other illness, children and aged people become easy victim of emotional illness. An emotionally sick person needs medication. Doctors, psychiatrics and behaviour therapists are to be consulted. Medication helps but only should be taken under proper guidance.

➢ Emotion literacy:

Emotional literacy is required for everyone due to following reasons –

- ✦ To detect emotional sickness, for self and others, at an early stage
- ✦ To find a non-medical solution
- ✦ To prevent the disease

➢ Emotional stability:

Balance among the emotions is essential to lead a healthy life. Alcohol, drugs, etc. often lead to emotional instability that often result in homicides and suicides.

➢ Emotional draining:

We often become victims of emotional draining. There are some people, who often try to offload their burden. In this process, they end up feeling better, leaving us emotionally drained. In the neighbourhood, workplaces, we often meet such people. Such people leave us tried and confused after we talk to them.

Anger and fear are very strong negative emotions. So, I will discuss them in depth and with ways to manage them.

➢ Anger

"Anger is the wind that blows out the lamp of the mind."

Anger is an emotional state. Joy, disappointment, frustration, etc. are called emotions. Anger is one of them. But anger is the most stressful.

Causes can be both – Internal and External

- ✦ Internal: Bad health like high blood pressure, headache, sleeplessness, restlessness, etc., suppressed emotions, volatile nature or character, etc.
- ✦ External: Irritation, noise, someone's foolish act, changed atmosphere, etc.

➢ Classification of anger:

To deal with anger most effectively, it is important to know the various types. So, classification is made based upon the anger felt by some people. Anger is of three types:

- ✦ **Concealed anger:**

The symptoms are a sense of energy loss, irritation and confusion. Note that it is real, but not as hot.

- ✦ **Blame yourself:**

It comes where you see your anger as a personal failing. May be blaming yourself for not being able to control your emotions.

- ✦ **Wrongly directed anger:**

Suppose the acts of your supervisor or customer make you angry, but you cannot blow it off. You suppress it temporarily but express your anger to another.

Your boss fires you, maybe because of your action. You suppress it for the time being, but express it when your subordinate comes to meet you. You fire your subordinate for nothing. The subordinate also does what you did. He fires his juniors. The junior goes home, fights with his wife and beats the children.

➢ Bad effects of anger:

When anger goes out of control, it is destructive. It ruins careers, it ruins relationship, spoils success. Most importantly, it affects health badly and reduces life expectancy.

Once, I had wrongly entangled myself in a heated argument with one of my best friends. That night I could not sleep. I was feeling miserable. All became the same only on the following day when we understood our mistakes and mutually said 'sorry.'

➢ Good effects of anger:

Anger is an expressed form of our suppressed ego. Therefore, it can be converted into a useful tool by effective application. This why probably it is said – "Anger is not bad, but acting on anger is bad."

Physiologists say that negative emotions like anger in a person, like the negative forces of the bar magnet, effectively repelled the forces of the negative powers of others.

➢ Anger management:

Anger management is to reduce both emotional feelings and the physiological arousal that anger causes.

Anger Management is a four-step procedure:

1. Feel the Anger

Try to feel the anger. Often we blow up because we do not feel the anger in time and as a result these powerful emotions take over leaving no further time to feel it.

ESP (extra sensory perception) or man's sixth sense is a wonderful gift. Sixth sense helps to analyse the situation and give us the caution on our expression of anger.

Some situations require patient control of our anger and some require momentary expression of anger.

2. Smile

Laugh off. Silly humour is also helpful. Do you remember the Hindi movie 'Munnabhai MBBS', particularly the character of Dr. Asthana acted out by Boman Irani. In the same way laugh off your anger and get relief.

3. Bring out the antidotes to anger

- Take a deep breath and think about the repercussions.
- Close your eyes and concentrate at your third eye, the point where both the eyebrows meet.
- Relaxation techniques, meditation, deep breathing, etc.
- Ignore and avoid. Switch over to some other topics.
- Count 1 to 10 internally.
- Jubrish talk – Sufi Saint Jabbar

4. Address the matter

Eliminate the cause of anger. This is some sort of permanent solution but not always possible to adopt. The easiest way to address the matter is to ask questions like "How do I respond? or What should I do?" etc.

➢ Life of an anger:

Depending upon the person, situation and the reasons, some angers are short-lived and some are live long. The person who becomes angry very fast also becomes calm fast. Such volatile persons seldom think about its repercussions prior to becoming angry.

➢ Old anger:

Fire in straw! See how it burns internally. No flame, no smoke, no external sign yet it may become devastating.

Similarly some angers are deep rooted, lying somewhere deep inside our mind (both conscious and sub-conscious) with no external expression. Anytime they can blow up. Old angers can be removed through the **GIGO** method of meditation or positive self-talk.

Anger in home generally do not last long. However, in workplaces, it can take weeks or longer to resolve, but with your inner thought-voice and your intention clear in mind, you can have more confidence and self respect. This can become the foundation to use anger for useful purposes.

➢ Fear:

Fear is one of the strongest negative emotions. Fear results in –

- ✦ Insecurity
- ✦ Lack of confidence
- ✦ Procrastination

There are two types of fear –

- ✦ Real and
- ✦ Imaginary

Reaction to fear is generally of the following types –

- ✦ Escape to a safe zone
- ✦ Encounter

Fear destroys happiness and relationship. Fears baffle and influence our decision, free expression, freedom, etc. and we accept injustice. Many a times, we shy away from good work out of fear.

Imaginary fear is more dangerous. Fear leads to anxiety, which in turn leads to irrational thinking. And this actually sabotages our solution to solve the problem. Imaginary fear magnifies the problem.

To drive imaginary fear, do the following:

- ✦ Get all the facts
- ✦ After carefully weighing the facts, come to a decision.
- ✦ Once a decision is reached, act!

➢ Wrong use of positive emotion like 'Smile' is very dangerous.

It is said – "Smile costs less than electricity but gives more light." But, smile should be thrown at the right place and at the right time. If not, what happens? Read this story.

Tapas used to work in a factory as a supervisor. He was an ever-smiling person. Wherever he went, his smiling face used to make him popular within a short period. Even in the most adverse situation also, he lightened the heaviness of the circumstances with his smiles. A new manager had taken charge of their factory. He did not know Tapas well. Once, when he was taking a round along with the investors of the factory, an expensive machine broke down. The machine was very critical to the plant and its shutting down meant heavy loss. The new manager and the investors were worried. At that crucial moment too, Tapas was smiling. It irritated the manager. His first impression about Tapas became so bad that it became difficult for him to tolerate Tapas any more. Finally Tapas, in spite of his very good nature, had to opt for a change in job.

The moral of the story is that smiling is a very good medicine. It can cure many ill relations. However its inappropriate use may be fatal. One must know the right place, the right moment and the right amount of smiling.

2.0 Power of Asking:

We barely realise the potential of the power of asking. It is one of the proven success methods. Ask your customer to know his/her requirement. Fulfil the requirement. You are a successful businessman. If you do not ask, you will not know what he/she exactly wants. There is a possibility that you may serve wrong things to him/her.

A shopkeeper sells an article at a predefined price. If you ask for a discount and he agrees, you get the article at a discounted price. You gain. If you do not ask, possibly you buy the same article at a higher price and you lose. In the same way, the teacher teaches; if the student asks a question, the teacher explains further; doubts are cleared. Knowledge level of the entire class goes up. Many are benefited. It is said even a mother does not feed milk to her baby unless it cries. See how simple is the power of asking.

My friend Sanjay is an efficient engineer. He knows his job as well as the jobs of others as the back of his palm. How? Only by asking! Whenever a doubt arises in his mind, he asks everybody – operators, technicians, peers, superiors, experts from other industries. He gained enormous knowledge by only utilising the power of asking to its fullest extend.

Someone has described it as an abbreviation. ASK → "A" "S" "K" →

→ "ASK", "SEEK", "KNOCK."

"A" is for ASK and you will know.

"S" is for SEEK and you will find.

"K" is for KNOCK and the doors of opportunities will open.

Suppose you want to buy some material. Ask for a discount, you will get the material at a cheaper price. Seek in the market; you will get the right material you need. Knock the suppliers, they will supply whenever you need. Asking costs nothing. So never shy away from asking.

The power of asking is dependent on 'how', 'when' and 'what' you ask.

How: it is the skill of using power

When: it is knowing the appropriate time of asking

What: it is the usefulness of asking

Use this power with skills and become powerful.

3.0 Mind Power and Will Power:

Mind power gives determination, the ability to persist, and the willingness to live with the head held high. A classic example is Gandhiji, who had a strong mind power that gave him determination and ability to encounter the British in a peaceful manner.

Another aspect of mind power is innovation. It is said that the mind is a mine. A mine of ideas! Just before committing suicide, an idea struck to the mind of young Dale Carnegie. Why not to interview a few successful people to find out the secret of their success. The result was a best seller – *How to win friends and influence people.*

Ideas are always floating in our minds. Only a few people can really encash them. Others simply forget or ignore them. What a great waste of mind power! Please note the following:

- The peculiarity of ideas is that they are short-lived. We forget them easily.
- Any raw idea has to be nourished so that it can reach an implementable stage. Our mental block comes in our way. As a result, we become judgemental and kill the idea forever.
- We very often share the ideas with negative people. These people always think that they are great and better than others in every angle. They always have nice explanations and reasons to prove your idea as vague and coming to a conclusion – 'It won't work out here.' Beware of these negative people and never share ideas with them.

To get rid of such situations, what I follow and recommend others to follow is –

- Always carry a pen and a pocket-size note book.

- Whenever an idea strikes your mind, just write it down. And gradually you build up an idea bank.
- Some ideas may apparently look silly. Never discard them but write them down in a separate note book to look into at a later date.
- You can discuss your ideas with positively charged persons and MasterMind alliance. Even if you get a negative feedback from them, never discard an idea completely.
- Refer to your idea bank. Some ideas are easily implementable. Implement them at the earliest.
- Within a short period of time, you will find many of your ideas have been implemented and they are really bearing fruit. This will make you happy and place you in a higher position.

It is said "Where is a will, there is a way." The will-power is the key to success and the source of happiness. It is an imaginary power that makes you really important. In fact, no one has ever succeeded without willpower.

Like changes and crisis, obstacles, particularly a situation like 'drowning man catches at a straw' are also great power generators. They teach you to live by struggling and create enthusiasm by supporting your willpower.

4.0 Power of Believing:

Power of believing gives birth to will. Will is more important than skill. It is said any success is 90% will and 10% skill. If you believe you can do it, I am sure you will do it.

Edison believed that if electric current is passed through a conductor, it would generate heat. If the flow of current continues to heat up the conductor, gradually the conductor will become 'red hot' and then 'white hot.' When any material is white hot, it radiates light. Hence, by passing current, light can be obtained. Edison's belief was so strong that repeated failures failed to stop him from discovering the electric lamp. This is power of belief. The attitude of persistence is mainly based on power of belief.

Power of belief is instrumental for the following:

- Generation of enthusiasm
- Confidence-building
- Development of persisting attitude
- Supporting willpower
- Identification of inner vision and mission of life
- Development of overall personality

.... And many other useful things

In short, one's success is dependent on power of belief.

5.0 Power of Knowledge:

Long long ago there was an old man. He had a fascination for having pets of various types. He had many animals such as horse, goat, dogs, cats, and birds of various species as pets. He had a big farmhouse to accommodate all of his pets.

One day, the king of the country visited his farmhouse. The king was very impressed to see his collection of pets. To encourage the old man, he donated some money to him so that he could buy some more pets. The old man thought that he had a variety of animals as pets in his farmhouse but had no chimpanzee. He longed to have at least one. A few miles away there lived a person, who used to catch chimpanzees from the jungle, then train them and later sell them at a higher price.

One day, the old man visited the chimpanzee-seller and selected one beautiful looking chimpanzee.

"What is its price?" asked the old man.

"One hundred rupees." the seller replied.

Though the price was reasonable yet the old man, out of curiosity, asked the price of another chimpanzee kept beside it.

"One thousand rupees," was the seller's answer.

"The next one?" the old man become more curious.

"Five thousand rupees."

"Oh! No!" the old man was surprised. A small ugly looking chimpanzee was silently sitting at one corner. He then asked the seller about its price.

"Fifty thousand rupees," the seller replied almost instantly.

"Gosh! Such a wide price difference! One thousand to fifty thousand! You must be kidding."

"Certainly not. All these three animals can perform three different tasks. The first one has a very sweet voice. It has been trained to sing as well as to attend to telephone calls. The second one is costlier because it has undergone a specialised computer training program and is able to handle any office job in an office. The third one cannot do anything, but can nicely take care of the first two."

The story is fictitious but its moral is deep rooted. It determines your market price. The third chimpanzee is costliest because it is powerful. It knows how to use others. In the same way, depending upon your capability to perform a job, your market value goes up. Your market value is more if you have earned the skill/power to use others well.

6.0 Power of Thinking:

A book had changed my life. '*Magic of Thinking Big*' written by David J. Schwartz. If you think big, you can achieve big. This is the power of thinking. What is thinking? Sit idle for a moment. A lot of thoughts will come to your mind. You can stress on some specific thought. Your vision is expanded further. You will be able to think beyond the usual.

Let me discuss about thoughts. Thoughts are ideas which come to your mind either spontaneously or as a result of thinking. It is said – 'Man is what mind is.' It is also said that mind is a mine, a mine of thoughts. Thoughts can be practical/impractical, productive/unproductive, good/bad and so on. However thoughts are classified as either positive or negative. Positive thoughts lead to happiness and negative thoughts bring destruction. This is because our actions are act based on the thoughts we generate.

The peculiarity of mind is that –

- It is highly volatile and it cannot think on one subject continuously for a long time.
- Negative thoughts come to mind easily.

Negative thoughts already generated in the mind repel positive thoughts and attract other stray negative thoughts. Thereby a piling up of negative thoughts results and a vicious cycle of negative thoughts is formed. Gradually, our mind become attuned with these negative thoughts and gets programmed negatively. Finally, the negatively programmed mind develops a stiff negative mental attitude.

Channelling of thoughts is very important. If you focus on problems, you will generate stress. If you focus on possibilities you will generate energy. Good thoughts produce ideas and the good ideas are the seeds of success.

The result of thinking can be anything – from ordinary to extraordinary. Any innovation or idea generation or discovering unique ways of doing a work is the result of vigorous thinking. Innovation is inner vision or fore-sighting! Thinking shows many things, which normally no one can see. Please note that thinking and worrying are different. Thinking is a good and productive habit, whereas worrying is a major health hazard.

A positive attitude is also the result of positive thinking. As per Shiv Khera, eight steps to building a positive attitude are as follows:

- ✦ Change your focus and look for positives
- ✦ Make a habit of doing it now
- ✦ Develop an attitude of gratitude
- ✦ Get into a continuous education program
- ✦ Build a positive esteem
- ✦ Stay away from negative influences
- ✦ Learn to like things that need to be done
- ✦ Start your day with a positive thought

The first and the last step emphasises directly on thinking.

➢ Conclusion:

Even if you fail to secure a so-called powerful position, you can gain power from any other unconventional sources of power and become powerful. You can achieve success and happiness with the true use of these powers.

Feel Good Factor ☺ 4

Belief is everything

If you believe that you can become happy, you will perpetually feel good. This is also known as "power of belief."

Belief is a powerful tool. It is the key to success. It creates wonders. But how can belief be a feel good factor? This is the most common question I always face.

I believe in God. I have faith in my deity. In times of adversity or whenever I am in trouble, I am scared, I am tensed, I am worried. I feel horrible. I pray or simply call my deity for help or chant his name. I gain mental power. I overcome the crisis easily. Smiles return to my face again. Then why shouldn't my 'faith' or 'belief' be a feel good factor for me.

Another example is Sakubai, our part-time maid. She comes to our house in the morning and goes back to her home in the evening. We trust her. Whenever we go for a long vacation, we entrust the responsibility of our house to her, simply by handing over the house keys to her. We never worry because we know that during our absence that trusted lady will take care of the entire house like her own.

Once Sakubai was ill, and it so happened that we had to rush to our home town for some urgent work. We could not hand over our house keys to anyone else as according to us none was trust-worthy. Three times, daily, we used to call up various neighbours to enquire whether everything was in order or not. We were so worried that we could not stay there longer. We had to return early. Such a thing had never happened earlier. The reason is simple – Sakubai's trust! Sakubai's trust did not allow worries to creep into our mind. Then, why should trust not be a feel good factor?

Belief is mental acceptance or something accepted as true. It is more than a mere suspicion and less than concrete knowledge. Knowledge is justified true belief.

Faith is generally a belief in a higher being. Trust also comes from belief. But it is a strong belief and complete confidence. Trust is a mixture of belief and confidence; but more of belief and slightly less of confidence. If you cannot believe, you cannot trust. Confidence comes from skill and experience.

Develop trust by trusting self and others.

Belief can be fact-based, real or imaginary. It can be right or wrong. What you believe need not be right. Superstition is a belief which is wrong, has no base and serves no useful purpose to the believer. The same is true of rumour. Rumours are usually a mixture of truth and untruth passed around by word of mouth. So, never believe in rumours and superstitions. They pollute the mind by providing mental blocks, generating suspicion, bringing down the self-confidence. Selfish people generate rumours for self-gain. Superstition is a tumbling block to progress. Positive thoughts bring happiness.

➢ Trust

"'A legacy of trust means a lifetime of reliability."

Mr. Kundanlal was a manager of an old government-owned factory, where annual increments of the executives were fixed and promotions were either time-bound or seniority wise. Under Mr. Kundanlal, there were two executives named Prasad and Hussein. According to Mr. Kundanlal, Prasad was trust-worthy but Hussein was not. So, Prasad was being entrusted with all difficult and important jobs, whereas Hussein was not utilised fully. This had being going on for a couple of years. As a result, both Prasad and Hussein gradually got frustrated and one day both of them revolted against their boss. The situation became so grave that Mr. Kundanlal finally was transferred and a new person, Mr. Zole, was brought in. Mr. Zole, on analysing the situation, realised that the problem there was due to trust and distrust. He distributed the jobs evenly by reducing the burden of Prasad and offering more challenging and trust-worthy jobs to Hussein.

A little girl and her father were crossing a rickety bridge. The father was scared so he asked his little daughter, "Sweetheart, please hold my hand so that you don't fall into the river."

The little girl said, "No, Dad. You hold my hand."

"What's the difference?" asked the puzzled father.

"There's a big difference," replied the little girl. "If I hold your hand and something happens to me, chances are that I may let go of your hand go. But if you hold my hand, I know for sure that no matter what happens, you will never let go of my hand."

In any relationship, the essence of trust is not in its bind, age, caste or creed but in its bond. So hold the hand of the person whom you love rather than expecting them to hold yours.

What should you believe and what you should not? Normal intellect is enough to distinguish it from rumours and superstitions. The following guidelines may help.

- ✦ Logical approach – check whether it is logically believable: possible or impossible to believe.

- Analytical approach – know the history, whether it has already happened earlier.
- What harm can happen if you believe or disbelieve. Our yoga teacher, Mr. Paranjpe says there is no harm in believing an 'untruth' if you gain. I would like to elaborate on the sentence. Hindus believe that a husband and wife relation continues birth after birth (*Janmjanmanter*). You may believe or you may not believe. It is up to you. If the belief improves the relationship between a husband and wife, then there is no harm in believing an untruth.

Rumours create an illusion, replicate a false picture. My friend, Paresh has a very bad habit of spreading rumours. I have seen people having faith in him gradually losing trust. Now his reputation is so bad that even if he tells the truth, people laugh him off thinking it to be a rumour. So a rumour is instrumental in losing friends, trust and happiness.

➢ Superstition, a tumbling block to happiness

Here is a story.

A wide psychological gap existed between Sarita and others. To Sarita, certain rituals and acts were her way of living; to others those were nothing but silly superstition. Since childhood, she had believed that the cawing of crows at odd hours or a black cat crossing our path were bad omens and certainly would bring evil news. Because of her superstitious beliefs, she often, became a laughing stock for others. Though this upset her terribly, yet she was firm in her belief.

She also believed that sneezing at the time of commencement of any auspicious work was an ill omen. Her belief was so strong that not only she herself followed it religiously but also used to enforce it strongly upon others. She would never allow her children to go out if she heard anyone sneeze.

Her husband, Avinash was the easiest victim of most of her superstitious acts. The poor fellow often used to be late for office because of her. Although all were concerned about her acts, yet the main problem was that none was ready to make her realise it. At least, Avinash did not have such courage! The children were too small to protest. And the neighbours, instead of guiding her, enjoyed the fun.

But one fine day strange things started happening. She discovered that her husband and children had suddenly become rebellious. She failed to find any specific reason for such behaviour. She intuitively felt the presence of some ill omen attempting to hog tie her family. She prayed to God because she was sure that the day could not bring any good news to her.

When Avinash was just stepping out for his office, Sarita could not control her sneezing. In fact, she had tried her best to stop the sneeze, yet it just happened. She tried to cajole her hubby from stepping out. But, he did not listen and walked away briskly, hushing her up by saying 'I'm already late …' She quivered with unknown fears, yet she could do nothing except pray for her irresponsible husband to return safely.

Shortly after that, when her daughter Rinky was about to step out for her college, somebody from the neighbouring house sneezed. She tried to convince her and said, "Wait, sit for a while and then go." The girl of a modern outlook, behaved contrarily to counter-convince her mother saying, "Come on, mummy! Don't worry. Nothing will happen to me. I'll return in a single piece." Her daughter's abrupt reply passed a chilling fear through her body. She could do nothing else except pray to God for forgiveness.

Soon her son Raju, who was suffering from a cold for the past few days, started for school, sneezing continuously. Like the others, he too paid no attention to his mother's repeated warnings.

Thus, all of her dear ones left home, one by one, dumping her into the deep ocean of worries. She was so distressed with anxiety and loneliness that she could not remain inside any more and came out quietly. When she opened the door to step out, a black cat came running and went cross the porch. She shuddered inwardly. She immediately turned back, as according to her, stepping out like that would invite further trouble.

She had a habit of a post-lunch nap. However, that day it got interrupted frequently because of the continuous cawing of a crow, which was sitting on the parapet wall of the neighbouring house. She tried to shoo it away, but it seemed that the crow was like her grown up children, no more afraid of her. Cold waves of fear ran through her body.

'Oh God! What will happen now?'

She was scared. She wanted to raise an alarm. No one was there to understand her distress.

She was so eager to know about Avinash and sound him about her apprehensions that she could not stay without ringing him up. But, that irresponsible guy, expressing his disgust in a loud voice, instantly put the receiver down.

> 'Now, what next? Nothing else can be done now. Hope all will come back safely!' She sighed.

Tears trickled out from her eyes. What else she could do other than weeping and waiting for all of them to come back? In order to get relief, she groped around the book shelf to look for a comic book. Instead, what she picked up was a book named '*Overcoming Superstitions*', gifted to her long ago by Avinash. Earlier, she had never felt like touching it. But that day, she found it interesting. She started reading it. Her fears and worries – all took a back seat for the moment.

She was so engrossed in reading that the jingle of the wall clock reminded her that it was six in the evening. She, once again, became dizzy with fear. She murmured,

'Normally, by this time, both Rinky and Raju come back. What happened to them? Why are they late today? I cautioned all of them repeatedly, these children of the new era don't care...Oh God! Save me from this crisis.' Almost at the same time ... 'Ding dong'! Sarita quickly opened the door. Raju, without giving her a chance to breathe, stuffed his report card into her hands. '87.5% Rank – first in the term exam!' – she grinned a smile of relief. A short while later, Rinky followed with a joyful smile. A foreign firm had selected her in the campus interview. The good news cushioned off Sarita's tension further. She gave a broader smile now and thanked God for saving her this time too. She was still anxious about her husband. Finally, she became fully relieved and completely tension-free only when Avinash returned home with a packet of sweets and a huge smile.

At night, Sarita, for the first time, felt that the tranquillity of the darkness had a zing of different kind. They had just planned for a pleasurable holiday trip to celebrate Avinash's new assignment.

To Sarita, the next morning was like the beginning of a new era. She was determined to start thinking and behaving differently. Avinash and the children, as usual left home, one after the another. She saw them off with a smiling face without bothering to prick up her ears to listen to others' sneezing, and finished all of her daily chores in a happy frame of mind. The lunch nap was extremely restful. The shrill caws failed to disturb her anymore.

Exercise:

What is the moral of the story? Do you believe in any superstition? If yes, what superstitions do you have? Did you ever experience any incident where you had ignored your superstition but the results were favourable? Just think and try to overcome your superstitious acts.

Feel Good Factor ☺ 5

Work and enjoy

Work is necessary to fulfil our needs. You feel good whenever your needs are fulfilled. So, any work, even a repetitive one, can be mood-altering and entertaining. The only requirement is to recognise the entertaining part of the work. Enjoy your work but always dream for a bright future. Forgetting the past, living in the present, and thinking about the road ahead are the seeds of happiness. You also must have a noble cause to feel good, a mission of your life and a vision as driver. Attain goals to feel better. Accomplishment, one after another, makes a person happy. Planning for future is essential. Discovering of the 'joy of work' is easier with Vision, Mission and Planning for the future.

➢ Work and enjoy

Nagappa, an industrial worker, is normally a jolly person. However, since morning he is in a quandary. The news of the death of a relative has upset him mentally. He thinks of taking leave but prefers not to, as he does not have enough balance. Unwillingly he goes to the factory, works hard there. His grief vanishes in no time to make him a happy person once again.

Shipra, a housewife, is yet to overcome the hangover of the previous night's quarrel, which she had with her husband. She takes up a long pending cleaning job. Her anger evaporates. She becomes normal again.

To both Nagappa and Shipra, work is a significant feel good factor. Tension, grief, jealousy, lust and many other bad feeling factors generate a lot of energy, which need a channelled way for discharging. Work provides such a channel.

There is a strong impression that people dislike work and they always try their best to avoid it. This is not true. I always believe that work is the most important feel good factor of life. Work means job, business or any other similar activity. The human body generates energy, both physical and mental, and work is the best outlet to transform such energy. So, work is a natural activity, an outlet of his imagination, a source of pleasure.

Contradicting it, my friend Sagar had once asked me, "Look at the world, industrial unrest almost every where, with various names like pen-down, strike, work to rule, etc., where working is so disgusting, how it can be a feel good factor of life?" My simple reply was, "Ask any able but unemployed youth, you will realise."

An unemployed worker expressed his anguish said, "I boil inside, but mostly I feel licked. I never imagined that the peace of my home is dependent on my job."

I still remember the day when, for the first time in life, I got an appointment letter. A lazy afternoon in a jiffy turned into a zestful day. Not job, only the news of a job changed my mood.

➢ How to make a boring job interesting?

Every housewife knows its answer. Prashant Maharaj is a temple priest. Dawn to night, he is engaged with the same activities, chanting *slokas*, offering *pujas*, and above all, day long fasting and one time eating at night. That too day after day, month after month. Is it not an exhaustive job? But Maharaj enjoys his job. According to him, it is the chanting of God's name that makes the most boring job highly interesting.

To make the job more interesting, following tips may be used:

- ✦ Clean up the area. Clean atmosphere changes the mood.
- ✦ Work at an ergonomically better posture.
- ✦ While working indulge in socialising, talking, singing, telling stories, gossiping, etc. In short, create a better and appealing social atmosphere (keeping evil effects of gossiping, rumours in mind).
- ✦ If you are to perform more than one job, select the dullest job first. In between, take up the interesting job. Boredom will be lesser.
- ✦ Sharpen your saw. Become more knowledgeable. If you know your job better, boredom will be less.
- ✦ Find out how important the job is to you and others. Be happy knowing its importance.

However, the best is to convert your work into a play. Think of a play where the reward is the work itself. When work becomes play, it becomes bliss. The man throws himself into the task with great energy and dedication. At that time, he realises that he also has aptitudes and abilities. Gradually, the ownership feeling creeps in. A dull job also becomes entertaining. An entertaining job is enjoyable and hence automatically becomes a good feeling factor.

➢ Enjoyable jobs:

Enjoyable work is required because a man cannot be a slave in a factory and a free man in his home. If he is unhappy and frustrated in his working life, he cannot be cheerful and happy in his leisure hours.

Work becomes enjoyable to us for various reasons. The reasons vary from person to person. Generally, work is enjoyable if it is of one's choice and close to one's heart.

Shivappa and Sridhar are workmen at a factory. They work in the same department and handle similar types of jobs. Shivappa is a very religious person. He reaches his factory early. He worships, performs prayer before he starts his day. He is always hyperactive for any religious or social activity in the factory. But he is a bit slow in his normal work. On the contrary, Sridhar is very sincere at his work but always shies away from religious or social activities. Shivappa and Sridhar have distinct choices and they enjoy performing their chosen jobs.

An enjoyable job, in general, should be –

- Non-monotonous: it may be any of the following –
  - To some persons, non-monotonous may mean a job filled with thrills and challenges. To many others, such a job may be fearful and not likeable.
  - Some prefer changes, but others may not.
  - Non-monotonous may mean fun filled jobs.
  - Non-repetitive or non-conventional
  - Problem solving type
- Sanctions enough freedom; less supervision and allows independent decision-making.
- Innovative, investigative or research type.
- Respectful to self and in the eyes of others.
- The job has competitive advantages with good future and career growth.
- A person may take up and enjoy a work if he gets encouragement from dear ones.
- The job does not create ergonomic or health-related problems.
- The work is not against religious and social belief.

My colleague Surinder feels an ideal job should have all the above components. A proper blend of all these components makes a job interesting and enjoyable.

What I have discussed is about an enjoyable job. To get a job of one's liking may not be possible, always. Hence, it is very important to convert a most boring job into an enjoyable one.

If you want lifetime happiness, learn to love what you do. Read the poem and realise this truth –

"When I was a lovely tiny boy, Playing with toy, was my joy.

When I, gradually, grew to a teen, Even in my fantasies, joys could be seen.

During the finale of juvenile trekking, Joy meant to me, raising toasts and flings.

When I sprouted even little further, I failed to collect joy from anywhere.

Later I grew to a big virile guy, I wanted to separate joy from enjoy.

When, I began combating to survive, Joy meant nothing, but a maze of life.

Gradually I became older and older, To me, joy was then, far from wonder.

I continued quietly to swell and grow, I found it again while digesting sorrow.

Next, I moved for effortful labour, Tried to extract joy from thither.

At the fag end of my tiring life, At last, I smiled when I realised,

I had unearthed the realm of joy.

That was nothing but **"Onus, work and enjoy"**!!!"

Yes, you feel good, as Kahlil Gibran said, when you walk to your goal firmly and with bold steps. It is unfortunate that most of us realise this basic truth at the fag end of our life.

Let us start with a story. The purpose of narrating the story is to understand how visionary thinking can change someone's life completely.

Once upon a time, there lived a king who had a big prosperous kingdom on the bank of the river Ganga. The king used to always remain unhappy and worried about the future of his kingdom after his demise, as he had no heir. 'Who will look after my kingdom after my death?' was his main worry. After a long thought, he decided that he would nominate that person as his heir, who had excellent planning skills for the future. However, he decided to keep his wish secret till the selection procedure was complete.

In order to do this, he announced throughout his kingdom that he would make any person, whoever willing, a king for a term of one year but with a condition. The condition was that at the end of the year the person would be left in the deep forest located at the north of the kingdom and if he tried to come back to the kingdom, he would be killed. The forest was dense and full of man-eating beasts. Leaving someone in the jungle meant sure death. No one came out to accept the king's proposal. After a long wait, one day a young man came forward and expressed his willingness to accept the king's offer. The king's men repeatedly explained the king's condition. But nothing could change the youth's mind. Seeing his firmness, the king crowned the youth as king for a period of one year and went on a pilgrimage.

The original king returned to the kingdom at the end of the contract period of one year. The youth handed over the kingdom to him. The king's men took the youth to the north to leave him in the jungle. When they reached there, they were surprised to see a newly built palace. The people were waiting at the gate of the palace to receive the youth as their new king.

How this could happen? When the youth came to power for a short period, he knew his future after one year. He, using his power, made a new palace, army and other necessities to convert the forest into a New Kingdom. So at the end of the year, when he was taken to the jungle, he faced no problem there.

Naturally, the original king became very happy seeing the foresightedness and planning of the youth and made him his heir. The youth was also very happy as it had transformed his life.

It is said the kingdom by the bank of Ganga ruled by the original king is "Benaras' or 'Kashi'. And the New Kingdom which the youth founded is 'Uttar Kashi', which is located at the north of Benaras.

My dear friends, I do not how far the story is true. But the moral of the story is that with proper planning and foresightedness (vision), you can achieve whatever you wish and enjoy a happy life throughout.

➢ Why do we work?

We work because it fulfils our needs. The young man, as mentioned in the story, accepted the offer because he wished to fulfil his needs. The heirarchy of human needs as mentioned by the psychologist Abraham Maslow are –

- Self-actualisation (Contemplation)
- Involvement (Joy of work)
- Esteem (Raising head and shoulder)
- Social (Need of friendship)
- Security or Safety (Job security, uncertainty of future etc.)
- Physiological (*Roti* – *Kapda* – *Makan* or body comfort)

The 'Needs' give rise to 'Wants'. If 'Wants' are not 'Satisfied', it will generate 'Tension'. 'Tension' gives birth to 'Frustration', the ultimate of unhappiness. In the long run it forms a vicious cycle.

Therefore, for feeling good, it is very important to stop tension-generation by breaking the vicious cycle and creating your own positive cycle. 'Motivation' can be one way. Motivation leads to positive behaviour change. And a positive behaviour change will result in improved performance. Better performance means better fulfilment of wants.

Someone gave a very good definition of happiness by saying – *'Working towards a worthy goal that demands our best is the secret of happiness'*. Vision, mission, objectives and goals are important because they are the driving force in our life. They motivate us to work. The proverb says –

"Chhoti chhoti bato se purnata aati hai! Lekin purnata koi choti bat nahi hai," which means small things creates fulfilment but fulfilment is not a small thing. Fulfilment of a dream is called success. Success brings happiness. How one can reach a goal or achieve fulfilment is a vast topic itself. The way to fulfilment is not a bed of roses but a path of thorns. On the way, one comes across a lot many hurdles which need to be overcome. Very often, one may fail; persistent tries turns failure to success. To feel good, it is necessary to celebrate each and every success and quickly forget the failure after learning a lesson from it. Persist to succeed. More persistence means more success. More success means more celebration. Each celebration makes you feel better. The frequent the celebration, the more you feel better and better.

There is a small caution. Persistence may destroy you. Persistence is a tool for success but one must know when to back off. It does not mean that you should not back off. Indefinite persistence without result may lead to frustration. Some people are often stubborn. Out of ego, they continue to persist. They do not understand the importance of backing off. They do not cut their losses and change course. As a result, after some time, their losses accumulate so much that they become easy victims of a vicious cycle.

➢ Goal:

Someone said – "Vision is passion." Vision is split into a number of goals. Goals must cover all important aspects of life. *Pundits* say a goal should be SMART – Specific – Measurable – Achievable – Realistic – Time-bound. I have a serious objection on 'achievable or attainable'. I believe goal must be something which inspires you. So, 'aspirational' is somewhat okay.

Conventional wisdom says you should work on improving weakness. What a terrible waste of time, talent and opportunity! A person becomes successful only by concentrating on strength. Moreover, such concentration gives happiness, as the person will be doing something which he/she likes. This is because everybody has a natural aptitude and interest in some areas and all of us love to work in our areas of interest. Developing natural talents is rewarding and motivating, allowing you to continually realise higher and higher levels of ability, achievement and success. Your goal will make you feel good about yourself.

Have you at any time noticed that any achievement, however small it may be, brings smiles on our faces? Accomplishment, one after another, keeps a person always happy. Failure can come in life, never be bogged down by it. It is all right even if you do not achieve. Persist till you succeed. Use various other feel good methods to boost up your spirit. The dream of success will uplift your mood.

➢ Vision and dream:

Once upon a time there lived a washer-man. He had a donkey for carrying loads of clothes. The donkey had to work hard and always obey his master, as the washer-man used to beat the donkey if any slackness was noticed in his work.

The washer-man also had a beautiful but foolish daughter. The daughter was very poor at studies. So the washer-man used to always rebuke her saying – "If you do not study well, I will marry you off to the donkey as no one else will marry you."

Once the washer-man, riding on the donkey, went to a market. At the entrance of the market, he freed the donkey for grazing and went for his work. Many other people also had left their donkeys there. Soon the donkeys become friends and started narrating their own stories.

The other donkeys felt very bad knowing the sorrows of the washer-man's donkey. They advised him to flee from the market and get rid of his sorrows forever. Surprisingly, washer-man's donkey refused to do so. Do you want to know why the donkey did not flee? This was because the donkey had a hope to marry washer-man's daughter!

The moral of the story is that an impossible dream is not a vision.

You must remember that you may have the most powerful locomotive engine of the world, it is useless if it does not run on the right track, the track that leads to the desired destination.

➢ History – The genesis of sorrows:

Thinking too much about a bad experience may make you feel miserable.

There are many people who have a bad habit of talking too much about their past life. They often claim that they had a glorious past but dull present and a very dim future. They, at times, are very proud of their ancestors but often do not hesitate to blame them for their present and future. To become proud of our forefather's and our good work is natural. Cursing the past is not the solution to any problem. History provides clues and solutions for the present problem. We can learn from history. However, it does not mean that we should only quote from history and always talk big. For our progress, our past is not very important. What we are presently doing is more significant. The most important is our vision and the action plan for the future.

Let us start with a story. Suman often goes to her office by taxi. One day, as usual, she took a taxi and asked the driver to take her up to the desired destination. The driver, who was a middle-aged man, started driving cautiously. Suman was extremely happy with his driving.

On reaching close to her destination, Suman softly tapped the driver on his shoulder from behind to tell him to stop. The driver was concentrating so much on his driving that the soft tapping by Suman made him tremble. As a result, he lost his control and met with an accident. Suman could not understand what could have happened to the driver to lose control totally. She so asked the driver the reason. What the driver replied was far from surprising! The driver was driving the taxi for the first time. Earlier he used to drive a hearse (dead body carrier). In that case, anybody talking or tapping from the back was not possible. The driver had been carried away by his past. When he was tapped, he felt some thing unusual.

In our real life too, we face similar situations. Quite often we are carried away by our past experiences, feelings and habits. Our mind is programmed that way. When our mind is programmed with nice experiences, our actions are good, but are devastating whenever it is other way round.

➢ Forgetting the past:

In our lives, we have been given a divine gift of the 'present' but we tend to indulge our masochistic tendencies and keep hurting ourselves by thinking of the pain of the past. Then the agonising past acts like a leech and disturbs our peace of mind, positivity and quietude, because we choose to remember it.

Actually we have the choice. We should let bygones be bygones so that we have inner peace. The past grief should be dealt with for some time and then totally removed from the mental canvas. But normally, we do the opposite. We harbour negative memories and irrigate the consequent resentment, guilt or regret and do not let go of our grievances, our anger, our tears and pain which eat into our system and make us sick. So it is best to bid 'bye bye' to hurtful bygones forever and live in a gifted wonderful 'present'.

➢ Think about the road ahead:

How the thrill of reaching a goal makes a person happy! I have my own experience. It was a hot, sweaty summer afternoon. I was travelling in a overcrowded bus. I had barely space to stand and breathe. It was probably one of the most unpleasant trips of my life. The bus was moving ahead at a snail's pace. Most of the co-passengers were expressing their displeasure. My mind was occupied with one of my ensuing projects. I could visualise the goal and dream about its achievement. I was thrilled to dream the success. In spite of the surrounding displeasure, I could feel the zest of happiness.

➢ Karma Yoga:

Karma Yoga tells how you can really remain happy through working. *Karma Yoga* or Dexterity in Action is based on the following:

- ✦ It is worship through work.
- ✦ Dedicated action would always have a touch of excellence.
- ✦ A true worker always shares because selflessness is the antidote for selfishness.
- ✦ Remain dutiful without expectation.
- ✦ Expect ingratitude.

Practice *Karma Yoga* to remain happy.

Feel Good Factor ☺ 6

Good habit confers good feeling

To get happiness, always ensure that you have already shed your bad habits and are continuously developing good habits.

Since childhood, Shyamsunder had developed a habit of taking notes. Wherever and whenever he finds a new thing or comes across a different experience or learns about a new subject, he takes down notes. Even today, his old notes serve as referrals or ready-made solutions to many problems. Similarly, Ghanasham has a habit of doing regular exercise and so he is always healthy, fit and happy. Both Shyamsunder and Ghanasham, with the passage of time, had developed their respective good habits which have placed them ahead of others.

A good habit has a direct relationship with other feel good factors. In fact, all other feel good factors are results of the adoption of a good habit. As for example, if you have a habit of working hard, you can really enjoy your leisure. If you have the habit of writing diaries, you can manage your time well. If you have the habit of thinking, you can innovate. And so on.

So, a good habit is a feel good factor for all of us.

➢ A bit about habit

What is a habit? Different philosophers have defined it in different ways. It is basically a repeated way of doing work, which is imbedded in human character. In short, habit is an established custom or a pattern of behaviour acquired through frequent repetition. We all are slaves of habit.

Although repetition of any activity, good or bad, for a considerable period gives birth to a habit, yet bad habits attract faster. It is said – "*Bad habits are like a comfortable bed, easy to get into, but hard to get out of.*" Therefore, any person who wants to become successful must have good habits in him/her.

Good and productive habits are strengths. They brings progress, success, and prosperity. *"Sow an act, and you reap a habit. Sow a habit, and you reap a character. Sow a character, and you reap a destiny."* A person with a good and productive habit gets others' respect. In short, a good habit attracts fortune.

➢ Some good and some bad habits:

Following habits are considered good and support one's progress and happiness:

- ✦ Getting up early in the morning.
- ✦ Reading books, taking notes and sharing knowledge (willingness to acquire skill).
- ✦ Managing time and relaxing.
- ✦ Following a routine and taking care of all sections of life.
- ✦ Nurturing one or two favourite hobbies.
- ✦ Attending *Satsang*, performing prayers, etc.
- ✦ Writing a diary.

- ✦ Never hesitate to smile. Smile even while talking on the phone.
- ✦ Helping peers and spouse in his/her work.
- ✦ Maintaining friendship and networking by occasional calls, e-mails etc.
- ✦ Not wasting money, food, water, electricity, etc.
- ✦ Abiding by rules and regulations.
- ✦ Participating in social work and charity.
- ✦ Going to bed early.
- ✦ Etc., etc., etc. There are so many....

Similarly, the following habits are bad and major hurdles to happiness:

- ✦ Smoking, drinking, gambling.
- ✦ Watching TV too much.
- ✦ Unwillingness to add skills and qualifications.
- ✦ Extravagant use of money and other resources.
- ✦ Wasting time and getting involved in some non-productive work.
- ✦ Being too materialistic and career-oriented.
- ✦ Neglecting other aspects of life.
- ✦ Talking too much especially when it is not required.
- ✦ Etc., etc., etc. There are so many....

Bad habits spoil relations, health, wealth, etc. Bad and unproductive habits are weaknesses. For a successful life and happy living, elimination of bad habits and adoption of good habits is essential. Bad habits can give short lasting pleasure but never bring happiness. If you are out with people who read books, listen to tapes, attend seminars, etc., there is a good chance that you will pick up good habits.

➢ How to know what are the bad and good habits you have

It is said old habits are hard to die. Through constant practice, one can win over one's bad habit. Before that, one has to know one's good and bad habits. To know them there are two easy methods:

✦ **Self-analysis:**

Take a sheet of paper and pen. Think for while. You know yourself better than others. Through introspection, you will be able to find out your strengths and weaknesses. On one half of the paper, write down your strengths. Suppose your General Knowledge is good, write it down. On the other half of the paper, write down your weaknesses. Suppose you are scared of public speaking, write it as your weakness. This is somewhat similar to SWOT analysis (Strength – Weakness – Opportunity – Threat).

✦ **What others think about you:**

If you can capture what others think about you, you will be able to know yourself better. This type of exercise is known as '360-degree feedback' scheme. Such exercise has to be done with very reliable and complaisant people and preferably under supervision of an expert.

In Winners' Club, we play it as a game. All the members say they are largely benefited by this. We normally pass a small chit to the other members participating in the game. The chit looks like this:

	Improvement Message from————to ————	
I feel		(emotion)
When you		(deed)
As a result of which		(emotion/deed)

A similar chit can be used by you to know what others think about you. Suppose 'Mr. A' writes about 'Mr. B' – "I feel miserable when you spit while talking as a result of which I don't feel like talking with you." This exercise will tell 'Mr. A' that he has a bad habit of spitting while talking and he must overcome this.

Only knowing strengths and weaknesses is not enough; it won't yield anything. You must prepare a time-bound action plan. Make separate action plans for strengths and weaknesses. Action plan for strengths must show the method to get benefit from the change and encash your strengths to their fullest extent, and the action plan for weaknesses should be able to convert them into strengths.

A secondary school student, Shanti is very weak in spellings. Whenever she misspells any word, her mother shouts at her to correct. Yet, she continues to commit the same spelling mistakes which she used to commit in her primary classes. In spite of her mother's nagging, why could Shanti not overcome her weakness? Nagging does not help anyway. It only complicates problems. People sometimes change themselves out of fear; but repeated nagging often makes them fearless.

➢ Action plans to cure bad habits:

After listing out the bad habits, the next step is treating them with proper antidotes. A few of such antidotes are –

- ✦ Use of negative emotions like fear, shame, etc.
- ✦ Confidence-building by adopting 'Fake to Make' philosophy.
- ✦ Use your willpower. Promise, make resolutions to discard bad habits and develop good habits. You may fail but never give up trying.
- ✦ Use of natural instincts like attraction towards opposite gender.

- ✦ Follow spiritualism and listen to religious discourses.
- ✦ Use specific therapy. Simple steps to give up smoking are explained later in this chapter.

But the best antidote for any bad habit, as said earlier, is replacing the old habit with the constant practice of a good habit.

Please note that both scarcity and affluence attract bad habits. Abundance, availability and temptation along with no knowledge of self-discipline attracts many bad acts, which on repetition generates bad habit. Hence, if you stop giving pocket money to a college guy, it does not guarantee that he will not develop bad habits.

A few examples are illustrated below to understand the effect of actions over habit:

❖ Fear cures habit

Mr. Sudhir Sakpal, a sub-inspector of police, was then posted at a criminal-infested area. He was very strict and known as 'terror' to his subordinates. One day, he along with his two constables went for a haul. On their return their jeep was passing along a slum area. On seeing a gathered crowd, he stopped his vehicle and instructed Havildar Manjunath to get down and find out the reason for such an unusual gathering. Soon Manjunath came back and said in a ludicrous way – "Saab, I got some valuable information, Saab!" Manjunath had a very bad habit of adding 'Saab' at the beginning and at the end of every sentence whenever he was excited. SI Sakpal glared at him which made Manjunath pause. After a long breath, he started a fresh – "I got some valuable tips from these crowds...." After this incident, Havildar Manjunath's bad habit of unnecessarily using the word 'Saab' had stopped permanently.

What made Manjunath give up his old habit? Firstly, Manjunath did not know at all that he had such a bad habit.

Secondly, it was due to fear of his boss. Lastly, when he came to know about his bad habit, he did not want to become embarrassed in front of others. Yes, fear often cures bad habits.

❖ Confidence-building to drive away a bad habit and develop a good habit

My friend Tarun Cabra had a peculiar problem. He used to take more time to pronounce the words starting with the letters 'T', 'C' or 'K'. At times, on asking, he could not even tell his own name. This used to put him in embarrassing situations because of which he started losing confidence.

I saw him at a personality development workshop for the first time. Like me, he too had joined there. At the ice-breaking session, all of us were told to introduce ourselves, one by one. When his turn came he stood up, and tried his best to tell his name but failed. Wanting to avoid becoming a laughing stock, he sat down without saying anything or looking at anyone. During tea break, when we interacted, his real problem became known to us that he faced difficulty in pronouncing his own name, Tarun Cabra.

Our facilitator, Mr. Bandorkar came out with a unique solution. He advised Tarun to add an additional alphabet or word before the words starting with 'T', 'C' or 'K'. It worked perfectly. At the end of the weeklong workshop, during the felicitation ceremony, Tarun could introduce himself well. He said – "I'm Ata-arun D'cabra ..." What he spoke may not be fully correct, but, he could continue his talk without much difficulty. It helped him regain his lost confidence. Years later, when I saw him again, he was a totally different person, a very confident person, free from any speech disability.

What Tarun had was not a real problem in the beginning. Though he had a little difficulty in speaking, yet it turned serious when he fell prey to his bad habit, which he could overcome after practice. Instead of bothering too much about the correctness of your speech, just speak up, the result will automatically follow. The formula for confidence building is 'imagine, pretend and act'. Often 'fake before you make' also helps.

Another friend of mine, Aroon Chanda was from a rural background and he had a genuine problem. He had a burning desire to talk fluent English. Luckily he knew the principles 'imagine, pretend, act and fake before you make'. In addition, he also knew how to resist negative forces. Wherever possible, he would start speaking in English. Initially, he committed many silly mistakes, grammatical errors, verb confusion, wrong pronunciation etc. His peers used to laugh at him. They tried to discourage him and would pull his leg. Aroon never bothered. He could insulate himself fully from all the negative forces. Now, he speaks the language with a convent accent. On the contrary, Sushil, a common friend of Aroon and mine, knows better English. Yet, he can not speak it well. This is because he was one of the leg pullers and never developed the habit of speaking English.

❖ Resolution – easy way to develop a good habit and discard a bad habit

A person can liberate himself/herself from the clutches of any bad habit with a strong willpower. A written resolution taken on New Year or any other day or on a specific occasion or during a religious rite can be a very good way to discard an old bad habit and develop a new good habit.

My friend Ashish wants to give up smoking. Every year, on 1st January, he religiously makes a similar resolution. He stays without smoking for barely one or two days. Thereafter, he is always tempted to take a small puff. He feels that his promise is broken and so, he starts smoking again. This has been happening for the past few years.

Chandan, another friend of mine, took a similar resolution on one New Year's Day along with Ashish. He, too, had a similar experience as faced by Ashish. However, Chandan tried his best to stick to his resolution. He started noting down every incident of promise-breaking. In the very first year, he had smoked 17 times, breaking his promise. The frequency reduced to 3 times in the 2nd year. From the 3rd year onwards, he became free from his habit of smoking. On the contrary, my friend Ashish still smokes as many cigarettes as he used to a few years ago.

We should always remember that the New Year is the time to turn over a new leaf. To some extent, people must believe in resolutions, irrespective of whether it is during New Year or any other time, because resolutions are actually just about preparing oneself mentally, as well as physically, to face the forthcoming year. It is like a dream that can turn into reality with sincere efforts.

New Year resolution is one of the important tools through which we can get rid of our bad habits. They should never be taken as old concepts or a legacy of the past. Of course, just making resolutions is not going to get us anywhere. The will to achieve is utmost important. But one should not bother too much about breaking the resolution once or twice. On the contrary, like Chandan, we should note them and gradually win over the bad habit.

➢ Easy steps to give up smoking.

Smoking is a bad habit. 80% of the smokers wish to give it up but they simply cannot. Something always prevents them from getting rid of this habit. A five-point program to get rid of smoking is mentioned below:

1. Off from your job for three days. Take 3 days' leave to start your own anti-smoking therapy.
2. Remain indoors or move to a place where you will not come across any smoker.

3. From morning to evening, drink plenty of water. Plenty means several bottles. Water flushes out impurities from your body.
4. Whenever you feel like smoking, put some non-intoxicating substance like clove, cardamom (elaichi), chocolate, peppermint etc. in your mouth. You can also have one or two antacid tablets. Take a doctor's advice.
5. Do meditation and light exercise. Deep breathing also helps. Swimming is very helpful.

Within three days, you will be free from the bondage of the habit of smoking.

➢ Necessity knows no law: Scarcity develops bad habits

Tamanna was an intelligent, cute and shy school-going girl. She was her teachers' favourite and the apple of her father's eyes, in short, lovable to most. Her parents were from the lower income strata where marrying off at an early age was the most accepted practice. But her father was not in favour of that. He had given her a lot of liberty and allowed her to study as much as she could. All were almost sure of her success in life. However, it did not happen so. Her life took a U-turn which nobody could have even imagined.

When she was about to sit for her school final exams, her father died. None of her orthodox relatives was in favour of continuation of her studies. She had to drop out from school and was married off to a person three times her age. Her demanding in-laws made her life miserable. They started scolding and beating her for trifling reasons. Because of weak support from parental home, where her mother was the only survivor, she had not much choice except to accept the destiny. Torture reached extremes when she delivered twin daughters. Finally, one day she was kicked out of the house. She had no other place to go. She started living with her mother and working as a domestic help. During this time, she realised that she was pregnant again. The news reached her in-laws house. They did not patch up with her. Her husband even denied the fact. Somehow, after passing a few more months of suffering, she delivered a baby boy. To meet her growing needs, she started working part-time in a beauty parlour. The income was still not enough to fill the mouths of her children. She longed to earn a little more. She hopped over to a tiny men's parlour as a beautician. Her shyness vanished in no time. She found an easy way of making money through tips and by entertaining customers in unusual ways. Tamanna, her mother and her children have now shifted to an apartment in a posh area. She now operates through her cell phone. Her poverty pushed her into the oldest profession.

➢ History is the genesis of many habits:

What is history? It is basically stories of our older generations, what they used to do, how they used to live, their past experiences, their advice for us etc. Experience is the best teacher. There is a saying that fools learn from their own experiences while the wise learn from others' experiences. Each of us, at times, is both fool and wise. Learning from one's own experience has a deeper impact. History corrupts our vision. Try to learn from history but never allow history to choke your thought process.

Remember the story of Suman? (Narrated in Chapter 5) How the driver had been carried away by his past? In our real life too, we face similar situations. Quite often we are carried away by our past experiences, feelings and habits. Our mind is programmed that way. When our mind is programmed with nice experiences, our actions are good, but are devastating whenever it is the other way round.

Exercise – call on your darling, Diary!

Try to learn from mistakes. Both, good or bad habit that you have developed or likely to develop has to be re-introspected for a better living in future. Take a pen and paper. Write down ten incidents of your past mistakes. Analyse them in detail. Write down the action you had taken on each occasion. What bad or good habit you have developed after each occasion; what actions should have been appropriate? Also write your plan of action for incorporating those actions.

At the end of each day, make a habit of noting down each mistake you had committed and try to win over them in future. Use your diary as a tool to get control over your habits.

➢ Good food habits also bring happiness:

Our food habits have a direct relationship with our feel good syndrome. Research shows that our mood often depends upon the type of food we eat. Happy, energetic foods promote the feeling of well-being by releasing feel good neurons such as Tryptophan, Serotonin, Dopamine, etc.

- ***Tryptophan:*** a mood lifting amino acid available in protein foods. It is a precursor to neurotransmitter.
- ***Serotonin:*** Helps the feel good factor. Low levels of this is associated with depression and anxiety. Foods that increase the level of serotonin are whole grains such as oats, barley, brown rice, millet and whole grain bread.
- ***Dopamine:*** Low level of this causes depression, while increased levels can bring about feelings of well-being. Dopamine requires vitamins B_{12} and B_9 which are more commonly known as folic acid. Food sources are fish and dairy products.
- **Chocolates** contain substances that mimic the effect of marijuana, boosting the pleasure you get from

eating them. They release ***endorphins*** that make us feel good. They are packed with anti-oxidants, especially dark chocolate.

- **Potatoes** are comfort foods and anti-depressants, rich in vitamin C. Whole and multi-grain breads enriched with vitamin B complex group too help.
- **Zinc** deficiency leads to depression. To fight depression, eat more alfalfa sprouts, brown rice, asparagus, mushrooms, turkey and radishes.
- **Bananas** are very good anti-depressants because they contain *tryptophan*, which releases the relaxing *serotonin.*

Combine all this with lots of water and eat your way to happiness. However, please consult a nutriotionist before you finalise your diet chart.

Feel Good Factor ☺ 7

Cleanliness, health and hygiene

You do not like anything when your health is not good. Health is not only wealth but also a feel good factor for us. However, cleanliness, and health and hygiene are always interdependent. Clean body, clean atmosphere and clean mind attract fewer diseases. Hence, I always prefer to club them together and consider them as a common feel good factor.

Suppose, Biryani is your favourite dish and you relish it whenever it is served to you. Suppose, while travelling from one city to another, you make a brief halt at a *dhaba* or a roadside food stall for lunch and you order a plate of Biryani. If the Biryani is served in a dirty and stinking plate, will you relish it in the same way you always do? Certainly not! This is the effect of cleanliness. You will eat even ordinary food to your heart content if it is served on a beautiful dining table and in shining clean crockery.

Like cleanliness, beauty also alters your mood. What is beauty? Beauty is a creation. According to an ancient Indian definition, 'beautiful' is that which from moment to moment is always new. It means a *change,* an important feel good factor.

A survey conducted by London Guildhall University of 11,000 people showed that (subjectively) good-looking people earn more. Less attractive people earned, on average, 13% less than their more attractive colleagues, while the penalty for overweight was around 5%. We always may not be in a position to create beauty. But cleanliness can make even an ugly item beautiful.

There can be *'Physical cleanliness'* and *'Mental cleanliness.'* 'Healthy Body' and 'Healthy Mind' are also each other's complements. Both are necessary.

By physical cleanliness, I mean cleanliness of body and surroundings. Physical cleanliness of body can be both internal and external cleanliness of our body. Physical cleanliness of surroundings means a dust-free, smoke-free, insect-free, and germs-free atmosphere where we stay.

Cleanliness also means everything is in order and there is a definite place for a definite thing. Nothing is placed shabbily.

Happiness comes easily through spiritualism. Your mind is always filled with positive and spiritual thoughts.

➢ Effect of bathing:

Just think of a tiring day. You have just returned from a daylong exhaustive work. You take a shower. You feel fresh. Bathing is an effective way to clean our body and refresh our mind. I still remember, it was a chilly night. After a night long travel, I reached Haridwar early on a cold and frosty morning. I was shivering and had become sick because of cold. An accompanying *sadhu baba* wanted to take a bath in the Ganga. Unwillingly, I too accompanied him. To my surprise, I felt so much better immediately. I had a different experience also. It was summer. After a long drive, we reached a holy place in Maharastra named Pali. There is a natural hot water spring. We were all very tired but decided to take a dip. Surprisingly, here too I felt extremely fresh. Our tiredness vanished even through a very hot water bath on a hot summer day. This is the result of taking a bath. Besides cleanliness, it has a direct impact on our mood.

Even a cold shower in winter and a hot shower in summer can alter your mood.

➢ Cleanliness and accomplishment

Is there any direct relationship between these two? My answer is 'yes'. Success is followed by cleanliness. The result of the survey conducted by London Guildhall University is an indirect indication. In addition, a clean atmosphere lights up the mood, isn't it? Yes! Cleanliness brings mood; mood to do good work and well-directed good work is the ladder to success.

In an unclean and shabby atmosphere, a lot of time is wasted on finding out the right material. Often important things are hidden under the heap of waste or unimportant articles. Hidden materials are often lost forever. Also, an untidy workplace increases our vulnerability.

Suppose you are invited to your friend's house for dinner. Delicious food is served in expensive crockery. But the room is shabby and very dirty; long cobwebs hanging from the ceiling. Would you enjoy the delicacy to your heart's content? Here the environment will make the delicious food distasteful.

➢ Concept of housekeeping: There is place for everything and everything in its place.

One morning, I found my friend Ashim ready for office, searching every nook and corner of his house for his car keys. He failed to remember exactly where he had kept them the previous night. According to his wife, it was an almost daily affair. Surprisingly, Ashim has no fixed place to keep his keys. Often he keeps them on the dining table, sometimes inside the showcase, sometimes in the racks of the TV trolley; he even keeps his keys on the bed, couches, rocking chair – nothing is spared. The result is a search operation like this one and the accompanying tension.

There must be a definite place for keeping certain items. The place must be convenient to the users. The advantage of keeping things in their right place may be any of the following:

- ✦ Enhancing mood – an aquarium in the living room or a window side flower pot
- ✦ Better time management – no time loss in locating the right thing at right moment.
- ✦ Minimising losses, damages, etc. while searching if the location of the item is known earlier.
- ✦ Lesser accident, better safety – incidents of tripping, falling, slipping are less.
- ✦ After all 'even a child can find it'.

➢ Mental cleanliness

So long we have talked about only physical cleanliness. It is important for a healthy body. For a healthy mind, mental cleanliness is necessary. The good ways for cleaning up of mind are:

- ✦ Fill up the mind with good thoughts.
- ✦ Always look for positivity
- ✦ Meditate and relax
- ✦ Observe silence
- ✦ Nurture a creative hobby
- ✦ Read good books
- ✦ Practice yoga
- ✦ Live with spiritualism
- ✦ Watch good and encouraging TV programmes

➢ Progressive Relaxation Technique: Relax! Relax! Relax!

Adequate rest and sleep is necessary for feeling good. How much is adequate? It varies from person to person. Simple relaxation techniques can be used to get good sleep. A very simple technique is illustrated below. Practice repeatedly for better results.

Keep your feet flat on the ground.

Hands on your thighs

Palms facing upward

Easy way to go into relaxation is to count 1 to 10

Take deep breath 5 times.

Mentally say 'Relax! Relax! Relax'!

Gently close your eyes. Let your eyes remain closed for some more time.

With your eyes closed, let your attention go to different parts of your body. Start from your right leg.

The toes of your right leg are now relaxing.

The sole of your right leg is now relaxing.

In between the sole of your right foot and the footwear that you are wearing, there is air space. Experience the sensation coming from that air space.

Your right ankle joint is now relaxing.

Now, shift your attention to the right knee joint.

In between the knee joint and the kneecap, there is air space. Experience the sensation coming from that air space.

Now relax your right thigh.

In between the muscles of your right thigh, there is the longest bone on your right side. Experience the sensation coming from that bone.

By now the whole right leg is completely relaxed.

Now start relaxing the muscles of your left leg.

Start from your left toes. The toes of your left leg are now relaxing.

The sole of your left leg is now relaxing.

In between the sole of your left foot and the footwear that you are wearing, there is air space. Experience the sensation coming from that air space.

Your left ankle joint is now relaxing.

Now, shift your attention to the left knee joint.

In between the knee joint and the kneecap, there is air space. Experience the sensation coming from that air space.

Now relax your left thigh.

In between the muscles of your right thigh, there is the longest bone on your left side. Experience the sensation coming from that bone.

By now the whole left leg is completely relaxed.

The right leg is already relaxed. Now the left leg is also relaxed.

Shift your attention to the muscles of hip joint. Relax them.

By now even hip joints are also totally relaxed.

Now concentrate on the muscles of your lower abdomen.

By now even the lower abdomen is completely relaxed.

Focus your attention to the upper abdomen and abdomen proper.

Inside your abdomen, experience how your stomach is moving.

By now, muscles of your abdomen are completely relaxed.

Now, it is the time for your chest muscles to relax.

Visualise the two big lungs inside your chest behaving like two big balloons.

The air is getting in and the air is getting out....

The air is getting in and the air is getting out.

Every time you breathe in, more and more oxygen goes in.

More and more oxygen means more and more replenishment.

Every cell in your body is getting refreshed and rejuvenated.
By now, chest is completely relaxed.

Focus your attention to your right shoulder joint.

As the right shoulder joint relaxes, the whole of right hand relaxes.
The arms, forearms, the finger tips – all are now relaxing.
By now the whole right hand is completely relaxed.

Now, focus your attention to your left shoulder joint.
As the left shoulder joint relaxes, the whole of left hand relaxes.
The arms, forearms, the finger tips – all are now relaxing.
By now the whole left hand is completely relaxed.

Both right hand and left hand are relaxed.

Now focus your attention to the muscles of your face.
Muscles around the mouth, tongue, throat, cheeks, nose, ears, eyeballs, eye lids, forehead – all are completely relaxed.

Concentrate on the head and skull.
The front of the head, the back of the head, the sides of the head – all are now relaxing.
By now the entire head is relaxed.

Now, it is the turn of the back to relax.
Visualise the muscles of the back and relax them.
Mentally count each of the bones of your back and relax the muscles around it.
By now the back is completely relaxed.

Your hands are relaxed!
Your legs are relaxed!
The entire body is relaxed!

For the next few seconds enjoy the silence within......

Now, mentally call back the numbers from 10 to 1. 10, 9, 8, ...1 and open your eyes.

At the end of the counting, you come out of this beautiful sleep, completely relaxed, like a battery recharged in all respect.

By practicing this style of relaxing, day after day, you feel better day by day.

Healthy Body:

A healthy body is necessary for happy living. Having a healthy and disease-free body is everyone's wish. I do not wish to enter deep into the topic because I hope readers do understand its seriousness.

Physical exercise, regular check-ups, timely medication, etc. are the various ways. Yoga is one of the recommended ways. The advantage of Yoga is that it makes both body and mind healthy. Yogis are generally happy. In a Yoga class, the instructor explained it very nicely in one sentence – "Before Yoga, body is straight and mind is flexible but after Yoga, body is flexible and mind is straight."

Feel Good Factor ☺ 8

Adaptation is happiness. Enjoy the change

For happy living, adopt the ABA (Alignment, Balancing and Adaptation) theory. This theory talks about balancing of needs, aligning self with the vision and adapting self with the changed situation.

Ignoring facts does not change the facts. So best is to face the fact and adjust self with the fact. Alignment, Balancing, Adaptation, etc are the various ways of accepting the facts and re-organising self with the situation.

For getting happiness it is essential to align yourself with the circumstances, balance your needs, and appropriately adapt with the situation. Harmony can never come in a non-aligned situation. An unbalanced person cannot remain happy for long. If the person cannot adapt him/herself with the circumstances, he/she will find himself/herself in the ocean of unhappiness within a short period.

Any change, however minor it may be irrespective of good or bad, physical or emotional, brings a lot of turbulence in our normal life. ABA is required to cope up with this turbulence. That is why this becomes an important feel good factor of our life. Actually change itself can become a feel good factor for us. However, its realisation may take a little longer time.

➢ Alignment:

According to my mechanical engineer friend Rangarao, perfect alignment and proper balancing is essential for moving machines, as it will give better life to the equipment. This theory of machines holds true for human beings too.

On getting D grade in PMS, my friend Harish promptly resigned from his job. At his farewell function, as usual, all spoke about his good qualities, highlighted his enormous contribution and good work done during his staying in the organisation. A lot of admirable words were also spoken about his recent achievements. At the fag end, when Harish's turn came to speak, he threw all in a very awkward position by posing a blunt question – "If I have so many good qualities, then why was I given D grade in PMS?" There was pin drop silence around for a moment. The SBU head finally lightened the situation with his good sense of humour. Readers, please note, here I am not doubting about PMS but highlighting its wrong but well-perceived interpretation.

Such incidents are not uncommon today. Similar stories can be seen in any office. In today's corporate world, PMS is the buzz world to decide an officer's fate. What is this PMS? Actually, its full form is 'Performance Management System' but has been nicknamed as 'Perfectly Manipulated System' due to various reasons.

My friend Arun once lightly said – "Your boss will manipulate your performance in your favour only if you are aligned with him"!

What is this 'alignment'? How does it influence our 'performance management system'? Whether it is limited to only PMS or beyond?

It took me a lot of time to understand the gravity and seriousness of 'alignment'

The term 'alignment', according to Management books, refers to consistency of plans, processes, information, resource decisions, actions, results, analysis, and learning to support key organisation-wide goals. Effective alignment requires a common understanding of purposes and goals and use of complementary measures and information for planning, tracking, analysis, and improvement at three levels: the organisational level, the key process level, and the work unit level.

But, such definition has very little exactness in context with PMS, where 'alignment' loosely means 'think what you are told to think and do what is told to you to do.'

My friend Karupaiya is a talented person, a skilled engineer. His organisation is proud of him. He is willing to sacrifice his comfort, holidays, even sleep for the sake of smooth working of the plant. Once, the Chairman of the company planned to visit the factory with a group of important dignitaries. Karupaiya's boss, the head of the plant, chalked out the plan for the visit in detail. Karupaiya was made in charge of housekeeping and was told to take care of the cleanliness of the plant. Karupaiya felt insulted because according to him, this was not a dignified job for a qualified person like him. Result? .....You can guess! Misalignment with boss ... and its ugly reflection on PMS.

Just look at the water pump set at your house. It supplies water to the overhead tank. From there, water is distributed to every part of the house. If the pump fails to supply water to the tank, distribution will came to a grinding halt in no time. An electric motor (or a diesel engine) drives the pump. Perfect alignment between pump and motor is mandatory. Absence of it may lead to vibration, noise and lastly, breakdown. When the pump and motor are aligned, pump-set operation is smooth. Any misalignment means problem!

The situation is similar at any workplace. Alignment is necessary even in real life. Friendship exists between two friends when they are aligned. Even enemy's enemy is friend whenever there is alignment. You may be highly productive but cannot become 'A' grade unless you are perfectly aligned with your superiors.

Think of any big family, preferably a joint one. Parents may have two or more sons. Ideally, parents should shower love equally on all the sons. But in reality it does not happen. Parents are also selfish in sharing their affections. The son who is more obedient usually gets more love. Isn't it?

➢ Balancing:

Like alignment, balancing is also very important. Out of balance is out of control. My friend Kashinath was very intelligent and hard working. He was an asset to his employer. He used to work 16 to 18 hours a day at a stretch in stressful conditions. He literally used to live with his work. His company elevated him to the rank of General Manager within a short span of ten years. But he could not enjoy his position for long. His wife divorced him, and family life got ruined totally. A short time later, he suffered a massive heart attack that resulted in his premature death at the age of 35.

What was wrong with Kashinath? His life was not balanced. He was a workaholic and had only one aim. He used to work without paying attention to any other needs of life.

My dear friends, you will find many similar cases like Kashinath's in your office, society and locality. Ask your doctor, he will show you a long list of such persons.

Balanced diet means a meal or snack that contains protein, vitamins, fat, carbohydrate, minerals, etc, adequately. Just as balanced diet is essential for our growth and healthy existence, in the same way, balanced life is required to live a mentally healthy life.

There are many other examples of balancing. Ask any housewife, she will nicely explain while preparing a tasty dish, how all ingredients are used in correct proportion to yield the desired taste. Absence of anyone will spoil the palette.

What is this balancing? According to my social worker friend Bharati Desai, life is divided into four major segments. They are your Professional Life, Personal Life, Family Life and Social Life. However, there can be more segments or sub segments. Look at the given figure:

Just imagine your life as a table and the four segments mentioned as its four legs. Can the absence of any one leg make the table stable? In fact, the table will be more stable if a few more legs are added to it.

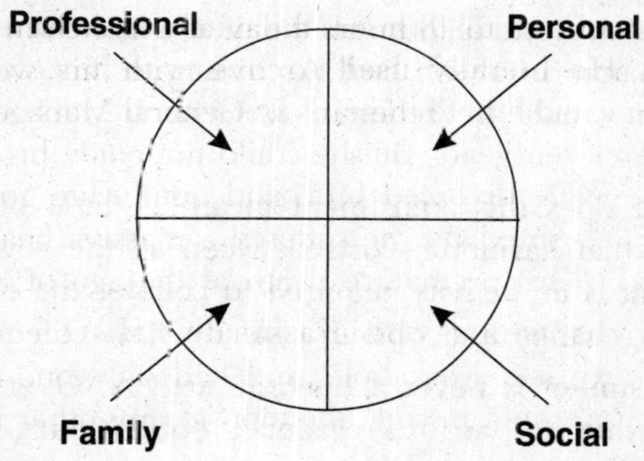

All the four segments of life have to be balanced for happy living

- **Professional:** Your occupation and career growth etc.
- **Personal:** Your religion, hobbies, liking, favourite pastimes, etc.
- **Family:** Your parents, spouse, relatives, etc.
- **Social:** In the society you live, your nation, community, etc.

Taking care of all the four quadrants of life and balancing them properly is a very difficult task. Needs or demands of each quadrant are unique and contradictory to each other. Satisfying one need may generate dissatisfaction in the other.

Bharati says, in most of the middle class families, right from childhood, overemphasis on profession can be seen. Parents believe that more marks means more success. Other aspects of the child's life are barely taken care of. Dealing with relationships is never taught. Such profession-centric society provides only a mechanical way of living.

➢ Adjustment:

After balancing and alignment, the machine is put on service. The mechanic is not satisfied. According to him, some more adjustment would be required for smooth running of the machine.

What does this adjustment mean? A little bit of fine-tuning so that harmony exists between all the components. Adjustment is an activity required to counter the turbulence caused by change and obtain a steady state of equilibrium.

Adjustment is never a onetime activity. Over a period of time, due to various reasons, equilibrium may get disturbed. Therefore, it is very important to know when to adjust, what to adjust, how to adjust and how much to adjust.

In real life too, adjustment is required for compatibility to ensure a happy living. Like machines, the turbulence in mind caused by a change has to be countered with the tuning of mind. These steps are to be followed:

1. Do not react immediately.
2. Identify only the positive aspects of the change.
3. Analyse how the change can influence your vision.
4. There will be certainly one or more factors that the change brings supports your vision.
5. Be cheerful and hang on those positive factors.

➢ Control:

Control is also an important factor closely related with alignment, balancing and adjustment. Control is disciplined way of doing things. You can't really become happy unless you have control on your action. Without the use of control, it is almost impossible to achieve balancing. Hindu and Buddhist philosophy has termed it as 'Sanjyam'. 'Sanjyam' is required in every aspect of life. If you have no control on your food, you are likely to fall sick. If you have no control on your emotions, you are likely to take wrong decision.

➢ Alertness:

Alertness is a must for perfect living. An alert person recognises the problem before it occurs and so he/she always has an edge over the others. Once upon a time, there was a loyal and sincere gardener. In a distant village he saw a beautiful plant which he picked up for his master. On the way back he met his old friend – the shepherd, who was carrying a goat on his shoulders. Both stopped under a tree, had a long chat and parted. When he reached the garden he was shocked to see an empty pot, the goat had eaten the plant! Moral of the story is that just being loyal and sincere is not enough – one has to be alert, otherwise even perfect alignment and balanced life will not take much time to go into the doldrums.

➢ Change can rejuvenate you:

Do you like a change? Do you go for a vacation? Try to recollect the last time when you visited a secluded hill station, away from the madding crowd. It was an altogether different life from routine. What for? Only for a change, isn't it? Look at any housewife, how carefully she alters the locations of household articles. She alone takes the trouble of lifting and shifting of heavy furniture, only for a change. Other family members immediately do not like change in location of goods but gradually accept it because it lifts everybody's mood.

Have you at any time solved puzzles or taken part in a quiz game? How interesting are they! Change brings a lot of problems. Best is to consider them as quizzes of life. Enjoy solving them. And feel good.

People look for changes. But surprisingly, when change is imposed on them, they resist. Why it is so?

Any change can cause worry because the fate, as a result of change, in not always known and the fear for the unknown is natural. But it is not so always. Often, no knowledge makes you courageous. But detailed knowledge is always preferred, as it drives away fear and makes you more confident.

Shantu, a five-year-old boy, was shy, always fearful and scared of everything. One day, while playing, he jumped from the terrace and injured himself badly. How did all his fearfulness vanish? From where did he get the courage to jump from such a height?

Nikhil and Anima are like any other new-generation working couple. Their only son, Bittu is growing in the care of their old housemaid. Little Bittu is very fearful. He is afraid of everything, from darkness to unknown persons. He is so fearful that he does not touch anything without asking his mother or the maid. In one fateful day, on getting a phone call, Anima had to rush home. This was a medical emergency. When the maid was busy with her household chores, Bittu had picked up one loosely capped medicine-bottle from the shelf. The doctors managed to save his life. But the question remained, how a fearful boy like him gained such courage.

In both the cases, the children did not know the outcome of their actions. Yet, they were courageous. Often, we act like these children. Courage without knowledge may become fatal. Changes often bring unknown fear. Hence, to drive away the fear, please try to anticipate the change, try to know about the opportunities that change will bring and grab those opportunities. Try to become more knowledgeable. Fear will go automatically. Never become ignoramus to changes.

➢ Change may become your turning point:

There are times when life forces us to make basic choices that could be life changing. These moments could end up becoming *milestones* or *turning points* in our lives. Often, a *breakdown* could very well be an opportunity for a *breakthrough.*

Let the change become the turning point in your life. Read this story carefully:

Since morning Sudha was in a quandary; anxious for the oncoming part of the day. To her, the day was more than crucial simply not because it was 'Open Day' at her son Rajat's school, but for many other reasons. Inwardly, she was afraid of getting scorched by the withering gaze of her friend cum neighbour, Kalpana.

Rajat and Ravi, Kalpana's son, are classmates. Last time, somehow Kalpana could heckle her when Ravi surpassed Rajat by only one mark. Now it was her turn to strike back... So, how could she remain undisturbed at such circumstances?

As the time passed, husband Avinash and son Rajat left one after the other. Loneliness of home started gnawing at her heart. She could not remain inside any more and came out silently, hiding herself from the preying eyes of her prying neighborhood.

She reached her only destination, Rajat's school, much before the scheduled time. Nobody else had turned up. She had no option but to wait outside. To pass time, she bought a magazine from a nearby stall and started flipping the pages. Her eyes suddenly fastened over an article 'Friendship and Jealousy'. She started reading it with great curiosity. Though she really liked some of the points mentioned in the article, yet it was difficult for her to immediately digest all of its maxims blindly, especially when Kalpana's hostility with her had already reached its height.

She waited outside for some more time and then entered the school on the pretext of meeting the principal. But, the principal pretended to be very busy and showed little interest in talking with Sudha. The principal's attitude was far from expectation. However, she left the cabin without showing any emotion but did not leave the school premises. The principal's attitude was still rankling her.

Slowly, the crowd of impatient parents started gathering outside the wrought iron gate of the school. It made her nervous. She tried to spot Kalpana in the crowd but she could not be seen around. Her mind was in a spin. What would happen if Rajat did not score well! What a shame! Kalpana was certainly not going to spare her the barbed comments.

She decided to stroll in the corridor. Fortunately, at that crucial moment, all of a sudden, her mind took a U-turn when someone called her from behind – "Aunty!"

Sudha turned back. "Oh! Ritu! What a surprise!" A pleasant smile came back on her face. A few years ago, Ritu had topped in the Board examination. Ritu was also a good gymnast and had taken part in various national level competitions. At one time, Ritu's father was her husband's boss at office. She had tried a number of times to get close to their family. Sudha was curious to know how this girl became a rank holder, as whenever she met Ritu's mother, the lady used to complain about her daughter not studying enough and wasting time playing.

Ritu was going away. But Sudha stopped her. She was more interested to find out Ritu's method of studying. She started talking with her without bothering to ask the reason for Ritu's coming to school.

As they went on talking, more and more surprises started popping up. Sudha was so amazed when she came to know that Ritu, even during her exam times did not stop her scheduled practice. She could not resist asking her –

"How could you manage to excel in both at the same time?"

"Aunty, my efforts always have been aimed at becoming good at studies. I'm continuing gymnastics side by side as an extra-curricular activity."

"If it's so, then why don't you give up the second to concentrate more on the first."

"Aunty, gymnastics is my hobby. I simply can't stay without it," Ritu replied.

"Don't you think that a hobby imposes on your main-stream activities?"

"No, not at all," Ritu protested.

"Why not? In the crucial final years of studies, when time really matters, hobby eats away a lot of your useful time. When every moment is priceless, nurturing a hobby means simply waste of time. Moreover, a hobby like gymnastics or any other sports or exercise, which involves a lot of physical activity, is no doubt tiring. I'm sure you could have scored more, if you would not have indulged in such extra-curricular activities."

Sudha tried her best to convince Ritu, but she boldly interrupted Sudha by saying –

"I'm sorry Aunty, you are totally wrong. I would have performed otherwise. Hobbies are like tonic. They refresh us. They remove our boredom."

Sudha was not in a position to spare that girl. She went on arguing –

"There are many other ways to get rid of boredom. As for example, if you are tired of reading literature, switch over to science. Whenever you are bored of mathematics, change over to history, geography and go on doing so. Take a short nap or you may even

walk for a change. You even can take some mood-altering drug. Therefore, one need not nurture a hobby or undergo physical exercises to get rid of boredom."

"A quick nap is indeed refreshing. Drugs are addictive and bad in the long run. Switching over from one subject to another often may help, but it may not be possible always. But hobby is something which builds up one from inside and has a long-time effect. I can give you an example from my life." Ritu paused a little then continued –

"Once I had tried this. I had given up my practice for a few days before my pre-final year exam. It was indeed suffocating for me. I could clearly realise that I was missing something. I was not able to concentrate on studies. That year my result turned out to be disastrous. So, I soon reverted back. I started my practice again. Slowly, there was improvement in my studies, and about the final year result – you are well aware." Ritu was firm on her logic.

"But, have you not felt at any point of time that a tough physical exercise like gymnastics is exhausting?"

"Over-exercise may be exhausting but proper exercise promotes a feeling of euphoria."

After a brief break, Ritu started explaining the benefits of exercise. According to her – "Exercise provides relief from stress, helps prevent coronary artery disease, delays ageing process, improves breathing efficiency, strengthens body, increases stamina and energy, reduces fatigue, results in positive thinking, better mental attitude and frame of mind and so much more." Sudha was really impressed by Ritu's explanation. She wanted to talk with Ritu for some more time. But, by that time, the school bell had already rung for the 'Open Day' to begin. On seeing the deluge of anxious guardians pouring through the main-gate, she had to say 'good bye' to Ritu and rush towards Rajat's classroom.

Sudha stood aside near the open window with the bunch of answer papers in hand and with great patience started examining them minutely. Her legs started shaking terribly. She never imagined such poor scores. If Rajat continued to perform like this, even getting a first division would be difficult. One or two curious mothers tried to peep in, but she immediately covered the marks. She could feel the presence of Kalpana at an arm's distance with her graze fixed at her, but she remained aloof. She returned the papers hurriedly and came back home without talking with anybody. She wept in despair.

Although this is just a story, yet it is very common to our lifestyle. There is always a Sudha living within us, trying to grab our entity. If you look around, you will certainly find many Sudhas in your neighbourhood. Let us see how this story takes a turn.

Sudha's husband Avinash, on return, was flummoxed. He was welcomed by Sudha's second phase of weeping. But, he, with his ever-smiling face, could change the atmosphere almost spontaneously. He patted Sudha and consoled her saying – "Keep patience, everything will be all right. Our Rajat will certainly come out with flying colours."

Inspite of Avinash's comforting words, she failed to sleep peacefully at night. All sorts of thoughts kept her awake. Ritu's victorious face and the article from the magazine appeared periodically in her mind. What did that girl say? 'Hobbies are like tonic' and 'exercises are always refreshing'. And the magazine? 'Jealousy pulls the person downward'. She could not remain in bed further. She wakened Rajat and the two joined Avinash, who used to go jogging in the wee hours.

They jogged up to the riverbank, where she first inhaled a chest-full of fresh air with delight. She had never enjoyed the morning like this ever before. She never had any idea that cool breeze could be so refreshing. She could see Ritu, at a distance, in a tracksuit taking her pre-practice round. She smiled a little and inwardly thanked her.

The days rolled on. The improvement in Rajat's performance was noticeable. So, they continued their early morning jogs even during his exam time. Their life gradually took a happier turn. By that time, Sudha had already given up competing with Kalpana, who too started responding positively. She never knew that delights of life could be achieved by incorporating such simple ways.

Both Rajat and Ravi had got admission in Computer Engineering. It was such a happy occasion that needed celebration. Kalpana's family and Ritu along with her parents were invited by Sudha. After a hearty dinner, Ritu's mother commented while looking at Sudha –

"You're really lucky to have such a nice son."

"All was possible because of Ritu," replied Sudha.

"Ritu?"

"Yes, Ritu had opened my eyes. After her explanation, I understood how physical exercise and hobbies are important for us. And because of this it was possible for me to put Rajat on the right track. I must say you're the luckiest to have a daughter like Ritu. May God bless her!"

Everybody present there ratified Sudha's statement by nodding their heads.

See how the story took a turn. Rajat's low score brought a change in her. Ritu's advice showed her a direction. As a result, a small incident in school turned to be the turning point in her life. This story tells us that:

- ✦ Any tiny point can become your turning point in life.
- ✦ To cope up with change, a change in mindset is necessary.

Exercise:

Identify *three milestones/turning points* in your life (from childhood up to now). Try to realise how they influenced your life.

➢ Change is precious:

Change can uplift us to make us valuable. A person I met in a fair narrated this story –

A man goes to a shop, picks up a beautiful cup and says "Oh! This cup is so beautiful!" Suddenly the cup starts talking – "O man, I am beautiful right now, but what was I before? Sheer mud! The potter picked me up, separating from Mother Earth. I cried. But the potter told me to keep patience. He spun me on a wheel. I was afraid. But again the potter said to keep patience. Then he put me in an oven. What a tremendous pain it was! But once again the potter said to keep patience. Then he applied paint. I did not like that. Finally, he brought me in front of a mirror and said – 'Now look at yourself.' Wow! I was surprised to see myself so beautiful."

The mud had gone through a series of changes to become a beautiful cup. The same way, we also face enormous changes which appear painful but finally lead us towards success.

I once had the opportunity to attend a workshop. The faculty was an IIM pass out. He told each one of us to introspect and write down a few of our past turning points of our lives and then read them aloud.

Ms. Saloni, a new entrant in our office, stood up. She talked about her young days, love, marriage at tender age, nagging in-laws, and finally broken marriage. In between, she was breaking down in tears. Finally, divorce became the turning point for her. She wanted to bring up her children with dignity. She joined a small firm. Joined college again part-time, for a degree. Gradually, she added to her qualifications and joined us for better prospects.

It was surprising that one of my friends Bhola, whom I knew for the past twenty years, was a rank holder in the school final examination. He did not show much of his talents while working. What made him lose his shine and remain mediocre? Did a turning point prove disastrous for him and pull him down.

At the end of the workshop, we could all realise that any change that appears as a curse might become a turning point of our life. Hence, instead of getting bogged down by it, it is always better to face it boldly and look for a worthy opening.

God is always good!

When a major mishap in our life can become a turning point, we say 'God is good'. Here is another real life story. My friend Sanjay had no sound economical or social background. After finishing high school studies, he, along with his friends, had come to Mumbai, to appear in a test to get apprenticeship as fitter in a reputed organisation. To become a fitter, more so to get a permanent job, was his priority at that time. After hours of travelling by train, when they reached VT station, it was late night. The selection was on the following morning. As they had not enough money to stay overnight in a hotel, the best option for them was to wait at the station and sleep on the platform benches. But unfortunately, Sanjay's bag that contained all the important documents (those required for selection) was stolen. As a result, Sanjay had to back out while most of his friends could sail through. Though the incident at that time had shattered him completely, yet it proved to be a major turning point in his life. Shortly afterwards, he found alternate sources for funding his further studies. Within a short time, he obtained a technical diploma and bagged a very good job.

➢ Change or to be changed:

Mr. Daga had been working for the past 30 years in the Vehicle Maintenance Workshop (commonly known as auto-garage) of a big company. He had joined as a trade apprentice in the department, gradually became trade helper, auto-mechanic, technician, etc. Because of his sincere and smart work the management seven years back, promoted him to the grade of supervisor. Barely one year back, after the retirement of his senior, he was made in charge of the workshop and promoted to the post of superintendent. A few days after this, the management decided to outsource some of its vehicle repair activities and hence, steps were taken to down-size the entire Vehicle Maintenance Workshop. Mr. Daga was transferred to the Mechanical Maintenance Department and entrusted with a section where similar type of activities are carried out. That was the beginning of the problems. Mr. Daga, could not accept his transfer to a different department. It hurt his ego. He was a soft-spoken person and rarely spoke out openly. Though he had never expressed his displeasure to anyone, yet his close friends could notice a drastic change in him. Gradually, his performance started going down. The incidents of absenteeism increased. A few months later, he suffered a massive heart attack. His problem became so acute that he had to take voluntary retirement on medical grounds. What actually happened to Mr. Daga? Why did such a nice personality shatter? The answer is – Mr. Daga could not cope up with the pressure of change that took place around him.

Nikhil*da*, as I saw him in my childhood, was a very mild chap. He was a displaced person from erstwhile East Pakistan. It is said that their family was quite well off there. Fate intervened and he lost everything after the Partition and had to struggle for survival in a new country. Surprisingly, he did not try too hard to overcome his financial difficulties. Finally, our beloved Nikhil*da* ended his life by consuming poison. Why did Nikhil*da* take such a drastic step? Why did not he work harder and try to earn a little more? Why could he not curtail his requirements? This was because he failed to tackle the change. The rapid change in his financial status made him mentally sick.

It is said once, during the British rule, an Englishman was asked – "Sir, in India what impressed you most?" The Englishman replied – "Indian girls." "But why, Sir?" "A little naughty girl's pranks keeps the entire village abuzz. But after marriage, the same girl easily adjusts in the new house and atmosphere, takes care of the entire family, survives on leftovers after feeding all, absorbs everyone's sorrows deep into her little heart and goes to bed after sending the entire house to sleep." How it is possible? The answer is change, which prompts her to respond positively and in a more responsible manner.

In all these three examples, the persons responded to change differently. Change is inevitable.

People have a tendency to say 'No' to changes. The cause and source of 'No' is the human mind. The human mind has a tendency for more comfort, peace, happiness, etc. Change is a new event, where often happiness becomes unhappiness, and comfort becomes discomfort and so on. And this is the prime reason for the 'No'. Fortunately, the human mind is highly adaptable. That is why, 'No' is a very temporary phase. It is seen in many cases that the 'No' to change is based on misinformation. Why is the human mind resistant to change?

➢ How to cope up with radical change?

To cope up with any radical change, a sea change in an individual's personality is required. The following behavioural tendencies need to be taken care of:

- Always remember, changes are not bad. In fact, they are often turning points and important feel good factors of our life.
- Program your mind to accept the change so that its opportunity part can be visualised.
- Know and develop your potential to maximise the benefit.
- Review your goal and action plan based on the opportunities and threats brought by the change.
- Get rid of your bad habits and develop new productive habits that are more suited to accept the change.
- Emphasise on your time schedule. Improve on time management, so that you do not take an unusually longer time to transform yourself according to the needs.
- Be assertive. However, situation-based controlled, aggressive and submissive behaviour also may yield results.
- Control anger and other negative emotions, which are generated by changes.

➢ Crisis:

Almost all of us, some time or the other, have faced small or big crises. Crisis means emergency. Any emergency creates a lot of panic and tension. Peace of mind is lost. Any such situation can be devastating if we fail to control our mind during this crucial period. Probably, learning from this book may be best tested during crisis.

Contrary to magic moments, crisis brings tragic moments. However, turning points may be either 'magic' or 'tragic' moments. Any crisis is an acid test of our mind.

➢ Obstacles:

Like changes and crisis, obstacles are also power generators. Obstacles are the opportunities. In fact, they are like knives. You have the choice of grasping them by the blade and being cut or grasping the handle and having a useful tool.

Exercise:

Take a pen and paper. Make a two-column table. On the left hand side of the table, write down the magic and tragic moments of your life. In the middle column, briefly write down your reactions and the actions you had taken up on each occasion. In the right column, jot down your learning from every occasion. Identify how many of these occasions had become turning points of your life. Just introspect and try to realise how significant that turning point is in your life. Be happy and thank God in remembrance of these moments. You will realise that you have enough reasons to enjoy the change.

Feel Good Factor ☺ 9

Relaxation and leisure

You feel better when you are relaxed. **'Manage time and relax'** – is the golden *mantra* for happiness. Follow a suitable and easy time management technique' so that you get ample time for relaxation.

Leisure is best enjoyed after hard work. So avoiding work is never recommended. Practice meditation and other relaxation techniques.

Sleep well and feel better. Adequate sleep is required for survival. But remember, only sleep cannot bring happiness.

➢ Relaxation:

Mr. Wilson is a brilliant engineer. He works hard. Within a short span of time he has risen to a top position and become SBU head. Almost daily he attends a number of meetings and parties with his various clients and VIPs where lots of alcohol and rich food is served. His day starts at 8 am but there is no fixed time for ending, sometimes it is midnight or even later. Even then, he carries a lot of homework in his briefcase and he keeps thinking about the next day's work. His life goes on like this and by the time he is 40, he has to shift to a new place – the Intensive Care Unit.

Take another case. Ramnath is a lazy clerk in a large private sector firm. He has a secure job with a fat salary but a nagging boss (according to him!) who keeps on finding fault with him. This makes him tense. On the way home, he fights either with the bus conductor or with a fellow passenger. Reaching home, he shouts at his wife, beats the children and picks up a quarrel with the neighbour, all for very minor reasons.

What is common with these two persons? They simply do not know how to relax.

What is relaxation? It is the act of relaxing or the state of being relaxed. More precisely, it is loosening or slackening and refreshing of body and mind. Work can easily be spoiled and wrong decisions taken if one is overworked and exhausted. So, relaxation is necessary, particularly after a tiring work.

A simpler definition is being at peace with yourself and your surroundings. It is a state of mind. Even when you are doing hard work, you can be relaxed mentally.

Relaxation is also one of the best ways of activating the subconscious mind.

➢ The most common allegation:

Most of the people claim that they do not find enough time for relaxation. Once, I read an article which highlighted the result of a survey. According to the survey, a major chunk of business executives say that although they are applying all sorts of time management techniques, yet they do not find time for meditation or going to the gym.

Strict following of time management principles will give you enough time for relaxation, which will rejuvenate you and make you feel better. Relaxation makes you cheerful and prepares you for the next round of action.

➢ Various ways of relaxation:

'Progressive Relaxation Technique', as mentioned in (Feel Good Factor no.:7) is a very good way to make you to feel better. The more you practice it, the more you will feel better.

There are various other ways to relax. Some of them are –

- ✦ Nurturing your favourite hobby, like gardening, writing, etc.
- ✦ Watching a football or cricket match or any other game, TV, picture, drama, etc, or listening to music
- ✦ Swimming or taking a warm/cold shower
- ✦ Singing, playing or riding or just strolling around
- ✦ Praying, worshiping, meditating or visiting a holy place or meeting a pious person
- ✦ Any other activities which refresh your body and mind

My friend Manish says that for relaxation, he prefers body massaging in a spa than any other thing. However, Muralikrishnan, another friend of mine, feels meditation is the best way for relaxation. Indeed, relaxation means differently to different persons. But, almost everybody feels relaxation is most enjoyable only after hard, tiring and stressful work.

The ways of relaxation, as mentioned above, have two distinctive varieties. One type calls for direct participation while in the other variety, we do not take part actively. As for example, while listening to music or watching a cricket match, we do not take part directly by singing or playing. Our participation is indirect. These may be called as indirect ways of participation or passive ways of relaxation. When gardening or meditating, our involvement is direct. Therefore, such activities may be called as direct or active ways of relaxation. Active ways are always better because in addition to relaxation, skill enhancement also takes place.

During relaxation, it is very important to have clear and channelised thoughts. If you focus on problems, you will generate stress even while relaxing. If you focus on possibilities, you will generate energy, which will generate enthusiasm for the next round of tasks.

➢ Relaxation, leisure and sleep:

Leisure is freedom from time-consuming duties, responsibilities or activities. It is also the time available for relaxation. However, relaxation can be a creative use of leisure.

Sleep is a natural periodic state of rest for mind and body. It is a type of relaxing. Adequate sleep is required for a happy living. During sleep, consciousness is completely or partially lost, although the brain remains very active. Relaxation is a conscious way of relieving stress. It can recharge our batteries of life.

Both under and extra sleep can be a feel bad factor, as it may make us dull and nagging.

A person can relax even while doing a job whereas simultaneous sleeping and working (except the use of subconscious mind) is not possible.

➢ Time Killers or Time Wasters:

There are two types of time killers. One type is where we ourselves are responsible for its wastage. In the other type, we lose out our precious time due to others' acts. Good time management techniques should address both.

Another two types are – easily recognisable and not easily recognisable.

Recognisable wastes are very common in nature and almost all of us accept them. There are various sources of recognisable waste. The commons ones are social, telephone calls, friends dropping by and conversations around the tea machine, etc. It would be foolish to eliminate all these non-work related activities completely.

An example of non-recognisable waste can be an afternoon spent polishing an internal memo into a Pulitzer prize wining piece of provocative prose. Other example could be an hour spent debating about the farewell gift to a colleague. Unfortunately, very few people want to recognise these as waste.

Among the major time killers due to others' acts, a meeting could be one, if not conducted effectively. Most of the business executives are its victims.

I had a long-time association with a social organisation. There, I experienced unique ways of wasting time in the name of 'meeting.' If a meeting was scheduled for 5 pm, the members rarely turned up before 8 pm. Hence, the time of the meeting was changed to 8 pm. People started coming in at 9 – 9:30 pm. Some members even turned up at 10 – 10:30 pm after having their dinner. Finally, we started fixing the starting and ending time of the meeting. The notice of the meeting used to read – "The meeting shall start at 7 pm sharp and end at 8 pm... the meeting will have the following fixed agenda... If discussion on any agenda consumes more than 15 minutes, that agenda will be dropped and the meeting shall move on to the next agenda." After this, we never faced the problem of late attendance.

Please note that there are some activities which may seem to be time killer/waster today but may save time in future. As for example, activities like planning for a job or coaching a person or reading a biography, etc, should be identified cautiously and used as time investors during the lull periods.

➢ Time Management: Find Time to Relax!

Truly speaking, time cannot be managed. But what can be managed are the activities and how we spend our time. The main purpose of time management is to eliminate the wastage of time, which can take place due to various controllable and non-controllable factors. It is a set of proven procedures.

Reasons for poor time management can be:

- Overconfidence
- Re-use or wrong use of a technique in a big project that is suitable for a small job.

By time management, we often mean Personal Time Management, which is basically a disciplined approach for the improvement of self. It even can be viewed as a management process that, like any other, must be planned, monitored and regularly reviewed.

Various time management techniques are available. What I follow, I have written here. Some of these techniques may sound crude yet they are helping me till today. The techniques are:

1. Use a diary:

What I perceive as the basic principle of time management is 'planning'. One hour of planning saves ten hours of toil. Take time to plan your days, weeks, months, years, etc. Use your judgement to identify and pick up the job priority-wise. This is possible only when you know what you want to do. That means a list of jobs or 'to do' list. So always remember when you measure, you can manage.

Long ago, when we were in school, Riju, one of my friends and very mischievous, one day asked me – "Indranil, do you know what does DIARY means?

I had seen my elders using the diary for calculations. It never struck my mind that the word 'diary' could carry any special meaning. Looking at my face, he tried to score over me saying – "**D**arling **I** **A**lways **R**emember **Y**ou (DIARY)". I was stunned but he went on smiling.

Years later, now I have realised how correct Riju was! A diary always remembers you. Even if you forget, like a true friend, your diary reminds you about your appointments, pending jobs, duties to which you are committed and a lot more. The writing of a diary regularly is one of the most productive habits. It is your 'to do' list, work sheet, and space for everything – calculations to lessons learned. But, a caution! Only bullet points should be written so that they are retrievable. Too much information should not hog-tie and drown you completely. With the help of a diary, you can manage your time better. Make the diary your darling. See how, even in changed atmosphere, it supports you. Use a diary as a tool to get control over your habits.

A diary, if used properly, is an efficient time management tool. Write your 'to do' list in your diary. It works as a good planner for rescheduling jobs, reminder of work, appointments, etc, also log your routines and daily activities to identify the time wasters.

2. Prepare & follow routines:

Make a daily routine and strictly follow it. A daily routine must cover all aspects of life. A typical daily routine looks like this:

6:00 hrs – get up

6:05 hrs – 7:30 hrs – Gym

07:30 hrs – 08:00 hrs – bath and breakfast

08:00 hrs – leave for office

|

|

19:00 – sit with children for their study

|

|

and so on

Once a routine is strictly followed, time can be found for all required activities.

Similarly, weekly and monthly schedules are also to be made. A typical weekly routine may look like –

Monday: call up at least 10 old friends

Tuesday: Visit temple

|

|

Saturday: Weekly shopping

Sunday: Eating out or picnic or visit a park

3. Multitasking (or Simultaneous working):

My teacher in college used to say –

"One job at a time, that done well,

That is the good rule that anybody can tell."

After college, when I took up a job, I found that the requirement is not one job at a time but multiple jobs at the same time. An executive is expected to manage more than one project simultaneously.

So, multitasking is one of the important time management tools. Multitasking means doing more than one job simultaneously. As for example –

- ✦ Reading, writing or meditating while travelling in a train or bus.
- ✦ Communicating through telephones while cooking.
- ✦ Listening to educative radio programs or CD or cassette during driving, cooking and other jobs.

The major advantage of simultaneous working is usage of time which otherwise will go waste. As for example –

Minu goes to college by bus. Her bus often comes 3-4 minutes late. She learned simple eye exercises, which she practices while waiting for the bus. This is also an example of multitasking, the efficient way to utilise time which otherwise will be wasted due to others' actions.

The only drawback I find in Minu's method is the chance of dust entering the eyes.

4. Right place for right material:

This is required to avoid running around and wasting time to find an object.

In the office, papers, files, register books, etc, should be kept in order of their importance, so that no time is wasted in locating them.

Cleaning up or file management of a personal computer helps in managing time.

In the home, there must be definite and separate places for keeping important papers, books, clothes, household items, repair tools, etc.

5. Advancing clock method:

I am often impressed by the working style of my friend, Geeta. She manages her office as well as family efficiently. She follows a very simple method. She advances her clock by 5-10 minutes in the morning and tries to complete her all jobs within the time shown in her clock. In the evening, she slows it down. She claims it gives her additional time to take care of her family.

I too am following this advancing clock method for a quite some time. It really helps to complete all the jobs on time.

6. Generate extra time:

Just like anybody else, I too at times face crunch of time. Though the idea of writing this book was conceived a few years ago, I was finding it difficult because of shortage of time. One day, I decided to get up half an hour early in the morning to write the book. Since then, I started waking up a little early. This method of generating extra working time worked miraculously. Within a few days, my book started getting a definite shape.

Half an hour daily means 3½ hours per week, 14 hours per month. That comes to 168 hours or 21 working days or 7 full days per year. Just imagine! By getting up half an hour early, we can generate time equivalent to 21 working days in a year. Is it not substantial?

The question is, will health be affected by getting up half an hour early? Certainly not! 6 hours sleep is adequate for the body. Most of us try to sleep more than required.

7. Let others work for you:

Delegation and out-sourcing are very effective time management tools. Delegate non-important jobs to your subordinate, children, etc. Out-source non-value adding jobs.

When you are entangled with too big a job, invite others to help. This will not only save your time but also helps to improve relations.

8. Cut down travel time:

Travelling is a major time killer. Do not travel unless it is absolutely essential. Make use of telephone, e-mail, fax, letter, etc. Similarly, first try to communicate on phone. Do not write a letter unless necessary.

9. Develop good habits and discard bad ones:

Watching TV, reading newspapers in detail, etc, do not add much value to our life. In newspapers, highlights and news of special interest and articles, which directly concern us should be read. Others may be ignored.

Another good habit is clearing desks.

10. Learn to say 'NO' whenever it is required:

My friend, Vidyadhar is a very busy, sincere and honest executive. Whenever a job comes to him, he does it with utmost care. His modesty and decent behaviour attracts more jobs. As a result, he is always on his toes and hardly finds any time for his own development.

Like him, there are many people who suffer, as they can not refuse jobs given to them. Never go on accepting jobs and piling them up. Soon you will be drowned and will find no time even for the most important job.

Conclusion:

Time management tips will vary for person to person. The way a college student manages time, the same way an executive cannot. The tips mentioned above are based on my personal experiences. To carve out enough time for relaxation, one needs to adapt more than one tip in combination.

Feel Good Factor ☺ 10

Self-realisation for contentment

Happiness is discovering 'self', the house of in-built happiness. Happiness is not in getting more but wanting what you get. That is why probably it is said that happiness is like a butterfly, the more you chase it, the more it eludes you. But if you turn your attention to other things, it comes and softly sits on your shoulder.

What is contentment? Ten poor men can sleep comfortably under one blanket, while two kings can not live in one kingdom. This is contentment. It is the state of being contented or a state that gives satisfaction. It is also a phase of happiness with one's situation in life.

In short, happiness is contentment. If you are content, you are happy. It is said that a contented man with a few hundred rupees is mentally as rich as a billionaire.

To have contentment, it is important to know and realise self. The basic of the subject comes from multiple questions like -

'Who am I?'

'What have I done so far?'

'What am I supposed to receive back as a result of my work?'

'Why should I at all get them?'

'What have I already received?'

'How many others have not yet received that?'

'Is it not a long list?'

'Why shall my achievement not make me happy?'

And so on.... The questions are triggers for 'Self realisation'. You will shortly realise that there is always something to be happy about. It makes you happy and this is called contentment.

Our elder son is shy, soft spoken and obedient. We do not have any complaint regarding his sincerity. Yet, my wife and I used to be always worried about him. The reason for our worry was that he was not very good at studies. Although he tries hard, he fails to score high in exams. This used to keep us worrying about his future and thereby making us unhappy. Recently, we acquainted with a lady whose both sons are spastics. This made us realise how happier we are compared to that lady. This is a real example of contentment.

Contentment is highly personalised. Self-realisation is one of the ways to know the extent or degree of contentment. 'Self realisation' is something that is a matter of feeling and cannot be taught easily. The essence of self-realisation can be experienced through –

- ✦ Yoga and meditation
- ✦ Observing silence
- ✦ Introspection
- ✦ Having a lot of fun

All these are interrelated. The realisation that my wife and I got came from introspection. For deep introspection, calmness of mind is required. Calmness of mind comes from meditation.

My friend Sagar, who is a strong believer of USP (Unique Satisfactory Point), opines that contentment is deliberate reduction of USP. Sagar may be correct to some extent. To become contented, often one has to bring down the USP to a lower level. However, it does not mean that the person should not be ambitious. A person must have a very high ambition and he/she must work towards its fulfilment. But he/she must remain content with whatever he/she gets as a result. And this is the real meaning of contentment.

According to me, USP is reflection of one's inspirational work. But contentment is a mechanism to become happy irrespective of the work done. An ambitious person may have very high USP, still can remain content. And contentment should never stand as tumbling block on the way to fulfil desire. On the contrary, contentment must keep one happy during the days of struggling.

So the *mantras* for contentment are –

- Know yourself in depth and more vividly.
- Remain dutiful without expectation.
- Expect ingratitude.
- Always remain 'owner's pride' and never 'neighbour's envy'. Be happy with whatever you have.
- Practice Karma Yoga.
- Never indulge in petty politics.

A winning attitude is always preferred. However, simply participation can often bring so much tremendous happiness, which even a victory cannot bring.

➢ God is good!

Here is a good story. Once upon a time, there lived a poor farmer. He had a very small piece of land, which he used to cultivate to make a living for his family, wife and a son. In spite of poverty, he and his family used to live happily. He had a group of neighbours, who used to envy his happiness by saying – "You are really lucky, farmer. You have a loving family and wonderful family life". The farmer's usual reply was – "I'm happy. There is not doubt about it. I really don't know whether I'm lucky or unlucky. God is great. Whatever He feels appropriate, He does for us. We are just toys in His hand". A year later, it did not rain properly. The crops did not grow. The farmer failed to arrange for sufficient food for his family. At last his wife died of hunger. His neighbour visited him and started saying, "Hey farmer! See how unlucky you are! Your wife has died leaving a baby son. How will you manage?" The farmer replied calmly, "I'm really sad today because I've lost my beloved wife. However, I yet can't say whether I'm lucky or unlucky. It's God's wish. He's great. I only know that I've to go on doing my duties. I've to take care of my son so that he never feels his mother's absence."

The days passed on. The farmer had become old and his son a stout young boy. The son was a very intelligent and hard working boy. He was very obedient to his father and started assisting him in his job. Looking at the duo, the neighbours very often used to say, "Hey old man! You've a very good son. You're really very lucky. You must have a very peaceful future ahead." The poor old farmer's reply as usual used to be, "I don't know whether I'm lucky or unlucky. I only know God is really good. He only knows what is good and what is bad for us. We only have to continue to do our duties."

The young boy gradually became an energetic and ambitious young man. He got a good job in the city and wished to go there. The old farmer had to agree and bid him adieu with tears in his eyes. The neighbours rushed to the farmer's house as if they were waiting for this moment and started saying, " Hey old man! What a pity! If the son doesn't understand the father's problem who else will? What a pity! Before leaving you, your son didn't even think once as to how will you live without him? The most irresponsible son! You're really unlucky." The old farmer was as usual and replied calmly, "I don't know whether I'm lucky or unlucky. I only know God is really good. He only knows what is good and what is bad for us. We only have to continue to do our duties."

Years later, the young man returned to his village permanently with a lot of money and gifts. The old man became very happy on seeing his son back home. The neighbours peeped in saying, "Oh old man! You're really lucky. You've a such a good son...." The old man's reply was as usual, "I don't know whether I'm lucky or unlucky..."

The young son used to like horse-riding. He used to roam around to far away places with his horse. He started getting matrimonial proposals from many well-to-do families. The neighbours continued to comment about old man's good luck. However, one day while horse-riding, the son fell down from the horse's back and broke his leg. He became partly disabled. Immediately the neighbours altered their views and blamed the old man's evil luck for the incident.

Around that time war broke out in the country. The soldiers from another country had attacked their nation. The king asked all young men to join the army and save the nation from defeat. All young people from the village had to join the army. But the old farmer's son was spared, as he was not physically fit. The worried neighbours came to the old man's house and said, "See old man, how lucky you are! When all of our sons are going to the battlefield, your son is saved, as he has a defective leg. We wish our sons also had something similar."

The story goes on. Things went on happening. The neighbours often envied the farmer, as he had good luck and sometimes felt pity for his bad luck. The old man accepted things as and when they came to him and remained calm all throughout.

The story illustrates that different things happen at different times but we should face the situation boldly as and when it comes and remain content.

Here is another story with a bit of a difference.

One day, a father of a very wealthy family took his son on a trip to the country with the firm purpose of showing his son how poor people can be. They spent a couple of days and nights on the farm of what would be considered a very poor family. On their return from their trip, the father asked his son,

"How was the trip?"

"It was great, Dad."

"Did you see how poor people can be?" the father asked.

"Oh yeah" said the son.

"So what did you learn from the trip?" asked the father.

The son answered:

"I saw that we have one dog and they had four. We have a pool that reaches to the middle of our garden and they have a creek that has no end. We have imported lanterns in our garden and they have the stars at night. Our patio reaches to the front yard and they have the whole horizon. We have a small piece of land to live on and they have fields that go beyond our sight. We have servants who serve us, but they serve others. We buy our food, but they grow theirs. We have walls around our property to protect us, they have friends to protect them."

With this, the boy's father was speechless. Then his son added,

"Thanks dad for showing me how poor we are."

Too many times we forget what we have and concentrate on what we don't have. What is one person's worthless object is another's prize possession. It is all based on one's perspective. It makes you wonder what would happen – if we all gave thanks for all the bounty we have, instead of worrying about wanting more.

➢ Politics

At a coffee table discussion over a controversial angle of 'happiness', once my office colleague Bharati commented, "Come on Ghosh*babu*! You must be kidding! In this era of rat race, where leg pulling and office politics are day-to-day affairs, how can an average person like us remain happy perpetually? If at all anyone claims to be happy, that person must either be a liar or a goofy." It took me time to make her understand what happiness really means, how contentment brings happiness, and the antidotes to deal with petty politics.

So far as politics is concerned, we can say that politics is an integral part of our life and deeply rooted in our day-to-day activities. "Man is, by nature, a political animal," as said by Aristotle. We face it almost daily. In this era of rat race, at one time or the other, almost all of us are victims of it. However its level and severity may be different.

The other name of politics is 'leg pulling'. Whether it is in the workplace or in a housing society or simply in the kitchen, the modes do not have much difference, and the impact is damaging.

Politics is basically used as a tool to establish command and secure a rigid position. Why do people indulge in politics with their own colleagues? The reasons are many. Some of them are – jealousy, ego, and ambiguity.

Jealousy is the major reason to indulge in such activity. In a stiff competitive atmosphere, the loser may initiate it out of frustration and the gainer may for securing his/her position and chop off the rival.

Jealousy may develop because of selfishness, over-ambition, a feeling of insecurity, superiority/inferiority complex, family or financial problem, poor upbringing, etc. Often a sadist mentality is also responsible.

When *ego* is hurt, wrong thoughts are generated. Ill will provokes wrong actions. Politics are ways for executing these wrong actions.

By *ambiguity*, I am trying to mean a situation where uncertainty is aroused from a not so clear instruction or from a non-transparent system. People may take help of politics to secure a firmer position.

➢ The antidotes:

We can find politics at even religious places, educational houses, charitable organisations, places of worships etc, those very places that are supposed to be places of unselfishness. Countering/tackling these petty politics is utmost important to feel good, for happy living and to become better.

How to tackle such problems? An antidote, as strong as poison, should be used. Suppose you are out for an early morning walk and you come across a barking pariah dog, what will you do? At first, ignore, then 'shu! shu! (Pacify)!' And finally if you are not successful, the only action left out is 'stone pelting'. If the dog is weak, it will run away; if it is strong it will attack and even try to bite. What will be your action then? Remember, a barking dog seldom bites. Flee out of fear or strike back with a bigger stroke. Fortunately workplace politicians are also like these dogs. They will only bark and seldom bite.

Hence, the best antidote to counter politics is similar. Use the **IPS** (**I**gnore – **P**acify - **S**trike) formula. At first ignore, then pacify and depending upon the situation, strike hard with an iron hand but never give up. Giving up means firstly, you are accepting your defeat and secondly, you are making him/her more powerful and lastly, creating many more victims. So expose the person fully so that others too understand his/her true character and motive.

As already discussed, politics comes out of jealousy. So if you are a victim of politics, always remember there is a hidden compliment associated with it.

Recollect the story of the Mexican person in related in the beginning of the book. The person is pretending to be happy because he is content. The moral of the story is – rat race that spoils your happy times may not serve any useful purpose in life.

A recent newspaper article reported that office gossip could be good for health. Some companies, in fact, encourage job gossip. However, experts feel that enough caution should be taken to be aware of hidden motives and sources of the gossip. People sometimes plant information to manipulate a situation.

➢ Enjoy the silence to feel better:

"Silence is the strength of our daily existence, a witness to everything: scheming politicians, rapacious bureaucrats and gossiping housewives." – R. K. Laxman

Observing silence triggers introspection and reflection. According to Hindu philosophy, it is one of the three essential attributes of a saint along with *balya* or childlike nature and *panditya* or wisdom. Great people in history had discovered the power of silence. Examples are many. Both Mahavira and Buddha had observed silence for many years. Sri Aurobindo had observed silence for 17 years. Gandhiji used to observe silence on Mondays.

Silence calms our restless mind.

➢ Inner voice:

Listen to your inner voice. It speaks the truth. It utters the words, which are based on ethics, morals, traditions and values. A decision taken based on inner voice is generally correct and has very high and ethical value and is also beneficial in the long run. Inner voice generally does not talk about short-term gain, of course exceptions are there, and precaution should be taken so that whatever you listen to is not polluted and no corruption is taking place. Observance of silence is the way to listen to the inner voice.

➢ Have fun:

Have fun to feel good. Fun makes life more enjoyable. It is enjoyable and a great tranquilliser. Always look for fun, even when everything is in doldrums, I am sure, you will get it.

A fun-filled life longs to live longer. It makes one realise how your life can bring a smile on your as well as an other's lips. I had seen one lonely old man, who always wished to die, as he had no specific reason to live. Once he became seriously ill. His son, along with his family, returned from abroad to see his ailing father. The old man got a companion, his little grand son. Fun and joy returned to his life again. Very soon the old man recovered from his illness. This is the power of fun and enjoyment.

I hope reading this small book was a pleasure,
I once again request you to mark your happiness level.

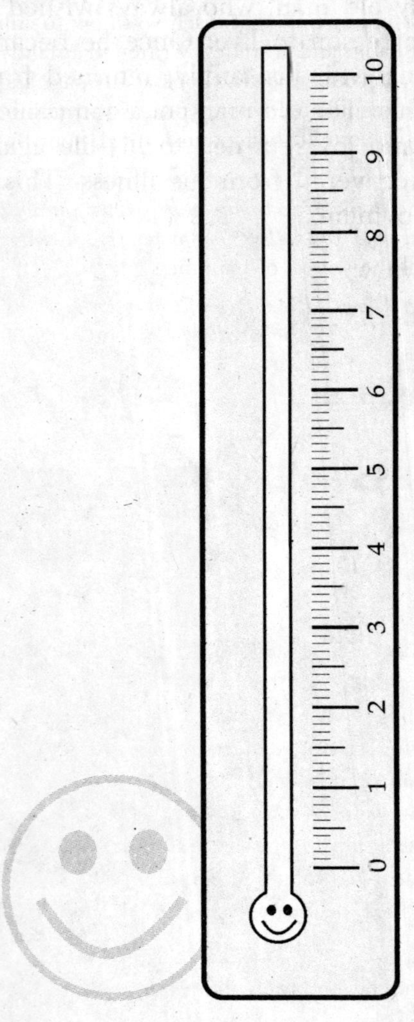

How to Remain Ever Happy

—M.K. Gupta

Everybody wishes to remain happy at all times, but very few discover true long-term happiness. Happiness, however, is a state of mind that can be attained at any time, provided we develop the right attitude towards all things in life.

This book contains 115 major guidelines, which include countless minor tips, that teach you how to cultivate the right habits and attitudes. Written in a stand-alone fashion, you could open the book at any page and read the specific guideline before you. As you imbibe and practise these teachings, you will notice your life being transformed, hour-by-hour and day-by-day.

To rephrase the opening lines in the book: *If you wait to be happy, you will wait forever. If you learn to be happy right now, you will be happy forever.* So why wait? Simply read this book and learn all the secrets of happiness.

Price: Rs. 96/- • Demy Size • Pages: 156 • Postage: Rs. 15/-
(Also available in Hindi & Bangla)

Secrets of HAPPINESS

—Tanushree Podder

We must look inwards as happiness is within us, like salt in the ocean

Happiness is a feeling of joy and gratitude that is more often than not fleeting. There are no magic mantras that will impart joy and happiness when recited continuously. It is only by developing a positive and cheerful attitude towards life that one can be happy. For peace of mind and contentment, we need to look inwards rather than outwards. We need to find peace within ourselves because it is not available through other means – no matter what price one is willing to pay. The book delineates ways and means to ensure happiness in every walk of life.

But the purpose of this book stretches beyond the visible endeavour of outlining codes of happiness. It also encompasses the need to bring in a little light in our otherwise gloomy lives. Many of the inspirational stories in this book will succeed in doing just that.

Price: Rs. 96/- • Demy Size • Pages: 192 • Postage: Rs. 15/-